Decentralization

To those leaders in education who blazed the trail for school-based management

Decentralization

The Administrator's Guidebook to School District Change

by Daniel J. Brown

CORWIN PRESS, INC.
A Sage Publications Company

For information address:

Corwin Press, Inc.
A Sage Publications Company
2455 Teller Road
Newbury Park, California 91320

SAGE Publications Ltd.
6 Bonhill Street
London EC2A 4PU
United Kingdom

SAGE Publications India Pvt. Ltd.
M-32 Market
Greater Kailash I
New Delhi 110 048 India

Printed in the United States of America

Library of Congress Cataloging-in-Publication Data

Brown, Daniel J., 1941-
    Decentralization : the administrator's guidebook to school district change / Daniel J. Brown.
        p.   cm.
    Includes bibliographical references and index.
    ISBN 0-8039-6005-0
    1. Schools—Decentralization—United States. I. Title.
LB2862.B77   1991
379.1'535—dc20   90-26172
                                                                CIP

FIRST PRINTING, 1991

Corwin Press Production Editor: Judith L. Hunter

Contents

Preface

An elementary principal in a large, urban district complains that he has no money to fix the school's adventure playground facility and can't persuade the board office to do it. A secondary principal in a suburban district is not able to get the right teacher combination he needs to address complaints about the math program because his proposal has bogged down in red tape. An elementary teacher is always refused when she asks the principal for science equipment. One school can't hire the kindergarten aide it wants desperately. Another needs a counselor but can't have that service to help its students. Yet a school board member observes, mournfully, that millions are spent in his district each year. Something is wrong. But the solutions to these problems were found in decentralization.

A principal in a decentralized district has just had her school budget approved. It amounts to $1.8 million. Her school has decided it will have 20 teachers for its 500 students this year. Among others, a reading specialist, a part-time librarian, and five aides are included in the budget. She has swapped some of her computer account money for professional development travel for teachers and aides. A laminating machine and VCR will be purchased. She expects to hire a mathematics specialist from the central office to offer a workshop on fractions for Grade 5. Her counterparts in the large secondary schools have even more discretionary latitude. Although they never get all that they want, these schools have matched their resources with their priorities. Something is right.

But to get from "wrong" to "right," a significant change must take place. This change is decentralization. If a district embarks on it, there is much to learn and lots of homework to do.

Why Is This Guidebook Useful?

Decentralization and its closely related term, school-based management, are "in the air." These ideas may have been kicked around in your district. That is because several highly visible reform reports, such as *A Nation Prepared* (1988) from the Carnegie Forum on Education and the Economy, *Time for Results* from the National Governor's Association, and *Investing in Our Children* from the Committee for Economic Development, all suggest that schools and districts be restructured. You may wish to play a part in the way this change comes to your district. Or you may just want to know how your role will change if it does. Regardless of whether you are a board member, superintendent, central office staff person, principal, teacher, support staff member, or parent, if you care about reforms designed to make a difference to the educational welfare of your district's children, this guidebook should help.

I have tried to avoid educational jargon but at the same time to introduce you to the terms used when districts decentralize. This book stresses the facts about decentralization. Although my enthusiasm shows, I have not tried to sell you on the idea. Rather, I have offered the pros and cons of school-based management in a non-technical way so you can make up your own mind. At the same time, I hope that you can find courage as you gain an understanding of the idea. But this guide is not a complete account of the decentralization story; you are asked to explore other sources. If you want to gain a grasp of decentralization in two or three evenings, this guidebook should suffice.

Acknowledgments

The following persons are thanked for their direct or indirect contributions to this guidebook: Fred Alexandruk, Hjalmar Arneson, James Cibulka, Emery Dosdall, Sharon Farinha, Leslie Greenway, Anna Lam, Tom Mah, Frank Martines, Lloyd Ozembloski, Mike Strembitsky, Austin Swanson, Richard Townsend, Jean Young, the anonymous reviewers, and the many students and others who contributed their information, thoughts, and reactions. Gracia Alkema of Corwin Press and Mitch Allen from Sage Publications are acknowledged for their most helpful advice and faith in the manuscript. Leanne Brown is specially thanked for her artwork.
It is also proper and fitting to express gratitude to those who provided support and ideas for my study of shool-based management. They include the Social Sciences and Humanities Research Council and the stalwart students—Darryl Craig, Eileen Hatlevik, Ros Kellett, Colin Kelley, Mark Stevens, Bob Tamblyn, and Dave Taylor.

About the Author

Dan Brown and his team of graduate students have studied school district decentralization since 1983. Armed with lots of questions, they interviewed principals and others in both centralized and decentralized districts. The people that they talked to responded with remarkable frankness about the joys and trials of life in education. This guidebook is based upon extensive research and current worldwide knowledge about school-based management.

Dan Brown undertook his graduate studies at the University of Chicago and then served as Professor at the State University of New York at Buffalo. Currently, he teaches in the educational administration program at the University of British Columbia. His best-known work is his book *Decentralization and School-Based Management*. Along with the continued study of decentralization, his research focuses on the ways in which schools attract gifts of time and money (voluntarism) and how schools seek private resources (enterprise).

STAGE I

EXPLORATION

When interest is expressed in decentralization, the first thing to do is to gather as much information as possible about the idea. Fortunately, the number of sources is growing. To help you find useful materials and ideas, a resource section is located at the end of this guidebook. The most important information will address the questions of what decentralization is, why it might be adopted, and why it may *not* be a good idea for your district. It will also discuss the appointment of a person to take responsibility for the idea and some warnings about how school-based management may be undermined in your district.

1 Brief Answers to Frequent Questions

You probably have some important questions about what decentralization is and how it may affect you. Here are the questions that I frequently hear and my short responses to them.

About School-Based Management in General

Isn't decentralization just a business model imposed on education?

Somewhat. The idea certainly does come from business. Educators are asked to set their priorities for spending money. The concept is well adapted, however, to the tasks of schools and does not turn them into businesses. Decentralization is a way of adapting schools to their environment, which has changed over many years.

Is school-based management democratic?

Not necessarily. The approach is not usually designed to increase the participation of teachers or parents for its own sake. Rather, it offers the hope that schools can be made better through the involvement of teachers and parents. Some forms of decentralization are more participatory than others; your district will need to decide which kind of school-based management it wants.

Will school-based management reduce the cost of education?

No. It should reduce inefficiencies, thus spending money more wisely. After decentralizing its utilities, one district found it was owed many thousands of dollars because of overpayments. But school-based management will not save money. The costs of education are not affected by this change in the administrative structure of a district.

Does decentralization resemble voucher plans?

In a limited way. They both encourage greater diversity in schools. The debate over vouchers, however, is an ideological matter because vouchers affect educational equity. In contrast, school-based management is seen as a pragmatic development that shells out resources more equally but allows personnel, equipment, and supplies to be allocated according to student needs within schools.

Is decentralization a new form of planning, programming, budgeting systems (PPBS)?

Only slightly. Each is an attempt to make education a little more rational, but that's where the resemblance ends. The intricate planning, programming, budgeting systems, introduced over two decades ago, were driven by experts using simple models. They were applied from the top down. School-based management, however, permits decisions based on local student needs to be made from the bottom up.

Will decentralization make schools innovative?

Don't bet on it. Decentralization offers more flexibility to innovate, but that does not mean that all schools will come forward with sparkling new ideas for experimentation. Some will take advantage of their newfound freedom to experiment. Most may not because no incentive is provided to innovate, only the resources to do so.

Does decentralization mean less central office influence on schools?

Yes and no. Yes, because central office *staff* personnel can no longer give directions to schools, which are placed in charge of their own affairs. No, because associate superintendents have direct control over schools. This means that schools report to only one person or position, according to the "one-boss rule."

Does decentralization mean that only schools will launch experimental programs?

Not at all. Many new programs are still initiated by the central offices in decentralized districts. But when most of the district's budget is given over to school control, schools have more opportunity to experiment.

Are schools more able to develop their own curricula?

Yes. All schools will have some discretionary resources that permit them to allocate funds for curricular development if they wish. Although constrained by state and district curricula, schools have the leeway to generate and try out programs tailored to their own students.

Will school-based management mean union busting?

No. Nonetheless, decentralization requires some elbow room on the part of collective agreements, particularly when union members request waivers to adjust the school conditions under which they work. The involvement of unions is an important component in the change to decentralization.

Does decentralization mean that parents control schools?

Not usually. If schools remain responsible to the school board and their parent groups are only advisory, then parents will not control all the power levers at schools. Yet, if the parent councils are designated as controlling, then they will direct schools in a similar way to that in which independent schools are governed.

How do districts change to school-based management?

Normally in three stages: exploration, trial, and commitment. First, districts explore and think about the idea. Second, they try decentralization for a few schools. Third, they make adjustments and adopt the idea districtwide. This guidebook is organized around the three stages that characterize the change from centralized management to school-based management.

About the Impact on Principals and Teachers

Will decentralization alter my role as a principal?

You bet. It will give you much more authority over the number and kinds of personnel and other major decisions affecting your school. It will also make you more accountable and increase your work load. And you will still need to conform to laws, policies, and contract provisions. Because no other role in the school district will be as affected as the principal's, a number of points in this guidebook are devoted to the principal's life under the "new order."

Won't decentralization turn principals into clerks instead of being instructional leaders?

No, not unless you actually want to become absorbed in accounting and related paperwork. Principals usually find ways to delegate the job of accounts management to their support staffs. Under decentralization, when faced with choices among important priorities, principals have more ability to exercise their pedagogical leadership if they want to.

Will decentralization reduce the number of mistakes made, particularly by principals?

Not likely. The buck stops at the principal's desk. Although some principals and their teachers will make mistakes, that's no reason to deny the majority the authority to make decisions. Principals, in consultation with their teachers, are able to make more important decisions under school-based management. Bigger decisions can mean bigger mistakes.

How do we know that principals and teachers can be trusted with money?

Research shows that school-based personnel in decentralized districts do make responsible decisions involving resources. My impression is that educators become a conservative lot when allowed to plan with money. Very few of them waste valuable resources.

My colleague, a principal from down the road, is both autocratic and political. How will he fare under decentralization?

He will have more authority to alter the direction of the school and the work life within it. At the same time, he will be held accountable for the results so all will know if his leadership style works. My impression is that autocratic principals do not consult sufficiently to make wise decisions under school-based management. Political principals, if they are averse to making decisions or keep changing the rules under which the schools operate, may reduce the performance of their schools.

Does school-based management mean that schools will have collegial decision-making?

Not normally. Teachers are not usually given a controlling vote over school decisions. Rather, the usual model for school governance is consultative, where principals lean heavily on the input of teachers but make final decisions and take responsibility for those actions, right or wrong.

Will decentralization increase teachers' work loads?

Quite possibly. Many teachers will be asked to participate in the educational planning process of their schools. When they accept this challenge, demands on time will grow and stress will be created as they help to decide on priorities and amounts of money to be spent on what their schools want.

Does school-based management mean that teachers may lose their jobs?

No. Their job security should not be affected. Note, however, they will be more accountable for their results because principals are held more accountable. Large-scale layoffs of teachers or support staff have not occurred because of decentralization.

Will school-based management affect a teacher's job very much?

Not greatly. The teacher's basic role will not be altered, but he or she will have more say in how personnel, equipment, supplies, and other resources are distributed within the school. My experience is that some teachers come forward and take an active role in school governance; others do not.

Will decentralization allow teachers to improve?

Not greatly. But if giving teachers a say in the kinds of people and things that their schools and classrooms need will help their students learn, then school-based management has the potential to help teachers become more effective.

2 What Are Decentralization's Main Features?

In a nutshell, decentralization

- is only one way to restructure a school district,
- is based on three important beliefs about schools,
- has two main dimensions, horizontal and vertical,
- has two main forms, organizational and political, and
- has a range of decisions to which it can be applied.

Decentralization and Restructuring

I am sure that you have encountered terms such as decentralization, restructuring, and school-based management before. It is important to understand what those terms mean and how they are used in this guidebook. For some people, decentralization is the same as restructuring, which is almost any change now being undertaken by schools. They are not exactly right. Fortunately, Ann

Lieberman and Lynne Miller, who are experts on restructuring, offer a ball-park picture. They provide five "building blocks." To them, restructuring is

(1) A rethinking of curricular and instructional efforts in order to promote quality and equality for all students.
(2) A rethinking of the structure of the school.
(3) A two-pronged focus on a rich learning environment for students and on a professional supportive work environment for adults.
(4) A recognition of the necessity for building partnerships and networks.
(5) A recognition of the increased and changing participation of parents and the community. (1990, p. 761)

Notice item number two. When enlarged a little to include districts, it focuses on a change in administrative structure, and that is what decentralization is all about. If we adopt this framework for restructuring, decentralization becomes a part of it. Just because a district decentralizes doesn't mean that it has been restructured in a number of other ways. But what does it mean to decentralize?

The word "decentralization" has a number of meanings. Sometimes it denotes that units of an organization are scattered geographically. Sometimes it suggests the breakup of large districts into smaller ones, as evident in New York City and Detroit during the late 1960s. I will not use the term in these ways in this guidebook. Rather, *decentralization* will mean the devolution of decision-making authority from central office to local sites. Notice the definition is a general one that may apply to any organization. But then what is school-based management? I will use the term *school-based management* to mean the decentralization of a school district or school's authority to make key decisions affecting it. Many authors have used similar terms, such as school site management and school-based budgeting. I will not worry about the distinctions sometimes made. Real budgeting changes imply changes in management. Schools may be called bases or sites. Although the basic idea is modified somewhat, it always suggests that a box of silver dollars is placed on the school's doorstep and the school has the authority to spend those dollars as it sees fit to educate the children whom it has enrolled. Throughout this volume, I'll use the words decentralization and school-based management interchangeably. Now let's consider what is behind these two ideas.

Three Key Beliefs Underlying Decentralization

(1) *"Some variability is good."* A social studies consultant in the school board office once had the difficult job of deciding how to distribute 90 globes of the world to 170 schools. He struggled with the desire to be fair to the schools that did not have globes, yet he also wanted to place them where they would be of most use. Then an unhappy question was raised: What if nobody wanted them?

The consultant tried his best to allocate the globes equitably among schools. In contrast, most persons can be persuaded that they could have been spread unevenly, and by the schools themselves. Some variability among schools is worthwhile. It is okay for schools to behave differently and for children to be exposed to somewhat different kinds of educational experiences. It is all right for schools to have variations in the kinds of professional help they receive, the levels of supporting staff they have, and the kind and quantity of equipment that they use. They don't all need the same sort of office copier, the same number of computers per student, a full-time learning assistance teacher, or the same number of teachers or assistant principals per student. To match resources to student requirements, some need more than the district average; some need less. Although the variability may make schools appear disorderly, this belief does not suggest that schools are outside of district control. When districts decentralize, their schools tend to spend their budgets on somewhat different priorities. Naturally, this means that what some schools have, others may not. This is okay. Some variability is worthwhile; not all differences are bad.

(2) *"Schools often know best."* A primary teacher requested that special counseling service be provided for a disturbed student in her class. She was told that the student would be placed on a waiting list because the elementary counselors were currently beyond the limit of their case loads. She noticed, however, that money was being spent on a district workshop in her school on the primary math curriculum, a topic about which she and her colleagues felt they already knew enough.

The evidence shows that district officials, remote from the classroom, often do not know what is best. School personnel know most intimately what their children need for their educational welfare. Principals, teachers, and the other schools-based professionals are the persons on the spot, working with their charges on a daily basis, so they are most familiar with their problems and their potentials. No one else has this close contact with the students and their families in the neighborhood environment. Further, these professionals have several years of education behind them; some have invested time and energy in earning specialized graduate degrees. All their preparation and experience gives them an excellent basis on which to make decisions about what resources (time, materials, and money) are needed for the particular students they serve. Not surprisingly, then, overwhelmed by the number of workshops that she was requested to take by the district, one teacher asked, "Why don't they just let us teach?" As far as she was concerned, her efforts were better directed to her students. If her district moves to school-based management, she will have more voice in how her time is spent. Although they may be local in a cosmopolitan world, schools often know best.

(3) *"Schools are usually trustworthy."* The school board included $100,000 in its professional development budget for teachers. But they needed to be encouraged to partake of workshops, both centrally and in their schools. The board believed that that money ought to be spent on professional development, otherwise teachers might not upgrade their skills. Yet after the district decentralized, the individual school budgets determined by principals and teachers were submitted. When the category for teacher professional development was added up for all the schools, it came to $400,000. What was wrong?

The board decided that the teachers were not willing to invest in professional development; they could not be trusted to do so. But when given the opportunity, schools rated the professional development function more highly than did the board. If left to the board, too little would have been spent on professional development. It appears that school personnel are trustworthy. People who work in schools have the best interests of their children at heart. When given the opportunity to spend money and not just get by with the resources given to them by the central office, principals and teachers will use the funds to buy the equipment, professional help, and other services in the best interests of their students. They take these purchases seriously and will not squander the dollars on frivolous expenditures or simply spend lavishly on themselves when given a lawful choice. When districts decentralize, I have found that principals and teachers (financially conservative people that they are) treat the public's money with great care and propriety. They put their students' interests first. No morally questionable uses of such funds have been reported to me. Maybe I'm too optimistic, but I believe that schools are trustworthy. The more centralized a district is, the less the senior administrators trust those in the schools.

These three beliefs constitute very important assumptions that are made whenever any organization decentralizes. The goodness of variety, the idea that schools know
best, and the belief that school people are trustworthy
must always be kept in mind and accepted. Otherwise,
forget it; decentralization should not proceed.

Two Main Dimensions of Decentralization: Horizontal and Vertical

According to Henry Mintzberg (1983), a leading theorist
in the study of organizations, unless they are managed
by a dictator, most organizations are already decentralized to some extent. He says that decentralization follows
two paths: horizontal and vertical.

When a school district is horizontally decentralized, it
means that decision making is shared among those at the
central office. The superintendent does not make all the
decisions, but has delegated authority to the assistant
superintendents, supervisors, coordinators, and other
specialists. Such is the case for most school districts in
North America. A problem arises, however, because the
persons in these specialist roles have authority for substantial budgets and also have the ability to direct school
personnel. Because of this authority and resources, they
are sometimes called "the blob." Although this group
contains some of the most able persons in the district,
they have authority but little responsibility because only
the schools have the responsibility for the education of
students. More on them later. Horizontal decentralization
is the norm for school districts.

Another way to decentralize is to distribute decision-
making authority vertically (downward) in an organization. As noted by Mintzberg and others, this form of
decentralization has been used widely in business and

industry in order to give divisional managers greater freedom to make decisions. Most school districts do not permit schools to have this kind of clout, as the district allocates resources to schools in particular forms (numbers of teachers, amounts of equipment) and schools do not have the latitude to make exchanges across accounts. However, under vertical decentralization, schools do have that authority after they have been given resources in the form of money.

How does a shift to school-based management change the degree of decentralization horizontally and vertically? Horizontal decentralization is reduced when direct control over schools is in the hands of only a few persons in the central office (the superintendent and designated associate superintendents). All others are moved to staff (advisory) roles. Vertical decentralization is increased when schools are given the go-ahead to select and deploy many of the resources they need.

Two Major Forms of School-Based Management: Organizational and Political

One school board member, seasoned in the ways of business, expresses the frustration of never seeing the "bottom line." Although she does not expect to assess the same balance sheet she is shown for corporate boards, she still would like to know exactly where the money goes. It seems to disappear into a giant pot and no one can identify how much the district is spending on any program. Not only can she not get a handle on the costs, she has no real idea of how schools are performing. Are the people who elected her satisfied with the educational services they are receiving, she wonders.

A concerned parent whose child attends a school in a large city would like to "make a difference" by being able to affect the important policies that shape his daughter's education. Yet whenever he makes suggestions to help her school, he is informed by the principal that all such decisions are made "downtown"—the school does not have command over them. When he hears that education is a top national and local priority, he can't fathom why parents are excluded from having much influence. For him "It's no way to run a railroad."

According to Maurice Kogan, a leading British scholar who has written extensively on governance in education, accountability takes two general forms. These alternative forms pose a significant choice for districts to make between two rather distinct forms of decentralization. One form is accountability based on representative democracy, where citizens elect persons to serve on school boards on their behalf. The board's authority is exercised through its administration and down to the schools. Under such conditions, schools would normally have parental *advisory* councils, but those councils do not direct their respective schools. Schools become fully accountable to one person—their associate superintendent who is in a direct line of authority to the board. This choice may be called "organizational" decentralization. Using the one-boss rule, it requires a clear indication of who is in charge of our schools. This form of school-based management is evident in Edmonton and Cleveland.

The other form of accountability usually permits control to be shared with a group of parents who (along with others) form a school directing council. Sometimes parents form the majority on the council; sometimes teachers do. Besides having the authority to hire or fire the principal and sometimes teachers, the citizens' group specifies many of the policies of the school. The form's basis lies in participatory democracy, where those persons most affected by public decisions are given a direct voice in how those decisions are made. This choice, which may be called "political" decentralization, requires a careful

specification between the authority of the school council
and the authority of the district's school board. This form
of school-board management, evident in Chicago, is advocated by Carl Marburger, author of *One School at a
Time: School-Based Management, a Process of Change
(1985)*. It is also supported by Brian Caldwell and Jim
Spinks (1988), two enthusiastic promoters of this form of
school-based management in Australia, who call their
model "collaborative school management." They believe
that the composition of a school governing council should
contain the principal, teachers, and community members. Others think that senior students, support staff,
and nonparents should participate as well.

What Decisions Should Be Decentralized?

Regardless of what form of decentralization is chosen,
districts are faced with an important range of options
when they ask the simple question, "What decisions could
schools make on their own?" The answers may be organized in a hierarchy. The first category implies the least
change and successive categories add to the kinds of
decisions included (see Figure 2.1).

Let's look at what's involved in Figure 2.1, the decentralization iceberg. The category of equipment and supplies (1) is quite simple, as it contains supply items that
are decentralized already. Equipment includes computers, copiers, lockers, desks, sports gear—all those material goods of school life aside from the building itself.
When equipment is added to supplies, schools can swap
between these accounts, a new possibility for many
schools. Although decentralization to this level is a significant change, it is not a pronounced one.

The professional personnel category, including teachers, assistant principals, counselors, librarians, and

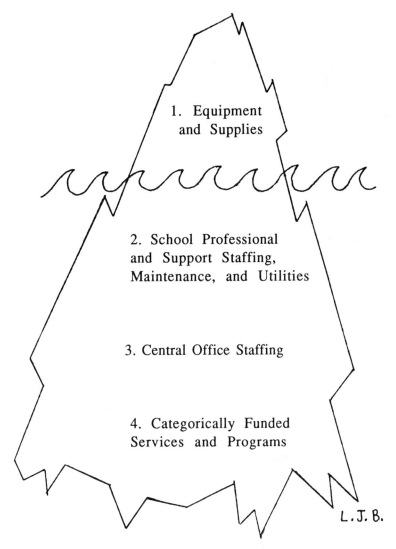

1. Equipment and Supplies

2. School Professional and Support Staffing, Maintenance, and Utilities

3. Central Office Staffing

4. Categorically Funded Services and Programs

L.J.B.

Figure 2.1. The Decentralization Iceberg

other special school professionals (2) is a big one, requiring much more preparation and posing more challenges. This category also offers much more flexibility because such a large percentage of school resources is consumed by salaries. The school support staff involves people in the roles of secretaries, clerks, aides, nurses, bookkeepers, and others essential to school operations. Remember that within a lump-sum budget, a school can determine the quantity and kind of teachers and other personnel that it wants. Almost as exciting, a school can swap personnel for material items and the reverse. For its part, maintenance includes custodial salaries, equipment, and supplies. When utilities are added, a school pays its own heat, light, water, and telephone bills. Utility costs, as we've been learning, can be high. One large secondary school's total came to $450,000. Decentralization that includes staffing is a major change for schools and districts and can be expected to have far greater effects than with equipment and supplies.

Next comes a composite group of services providing the help that schools require (3). This category includes all the valuable within-district services provided by coordinators and subject specialists in the central office that may be placed on a user-pay arrangement with schools. That help can be in the form of professional development, staff training, or sometimes direct assistance with problems. The decentralization of these functions requires careful planning with central office personnel, school persons, union groups, and private companies. Such services are offered to schools but the schools pay for them. Flexibility is considerably amplified with the inclusion of these items and, again, the ability to exchange dollars across accounts is a significant way to increase the ability of schools to meet the range of student needs.

Last are the categorically funded services that are not usually associated with schools but that schools need (4). They include allocations that cover special education and federal programs. It may not be legally possible to decentralize some of these in certain jurisdictions, but in others this can be and has been done. Once more, the possibilities of discretion in matching resources to student needs are enhanced considerably. What about those decisions that do not pass the test? Schools really cannot make them on their own. Most districts with school-based management reserve a set of decisions that are either logically centralized because they are seen as districtwide or that remain centralized for the sake of efficiency. Among the logically centralized are school construction, major renovations, general district policy, teacher transfers, and articulation with senior governments. Among the ones centralized for efficiency are most purchases, payroll, collective agreements, daily transportation, and closure of schools because of weather conditions.

Summary: What Is the Core of Decentralization?

Decentralization is only a part of the restructuring phenomenon. The processes of restructuring can also involve major curricular and instructional changes and significant alterations to the teaching profession. Decentralization itself is the devolution of authority; school-based management means that the schools make the decisions on key matters that affect them. Decentralization and school-based management are used synonymously in this guidebook.

School-based management may be seen as grounded on certain assumptions — certain beliefs about the need for variety, the idea that schools know best, and that school personnel are by and large trustworthy. Remember these tenets; decentralization cannot really proceed without their recognition.

Districts face substantial choices when they contemplate decentralization. Will the parents, teachers, or the school board dominate the schools? And how much decentralization is desired? Is it wiser to adopt the idea a little or a lot?

Your exploration of decentralization needs to tell you not just what it is, but what it does. School-based management may be expected to provide an increase in flexibility, more accountability, and, quite likely, greater productivity for schools. As one associate superintendent said, "It takes off their chains." Let's look at each outcome in turn.

3 Why Decentralize a School District?

In a nutshell, districts decentralize because

- school flexibility of decision making grows;
- accountability to the school board or parent/teacher council increases;
- school productivity is likely to go up.

More Flexibility of Decision Making

A principal once had a plan to enlarge the library space with new shelves. Yet his attempts to have the renovations office put in the new shelves failed: No funds were available. Yet, one day, without warning, a crew arrived to take off the old school doors and replace them with new ones. The principal's reaction was, "We don't need new doors, the old ones are just fine." But he was told that door replacement was a periodic matter and his school's time had come. In a flash of insight known only to principals, he responded, "Give me the old doors!" Sorry, he was told, the policy was to return them to the renovations office.

Unfortunately, these kinds of events are the norm in centralized districts. Schools are not permitted to switch from unwanted to desired resources for the benefit of their students. That rule applies to equipment, mainte- nance, professional staffing, support staffing, and other categories. It is as if all accounts were isolated (see Fig- ure 3.1). Some principals rebel and break the rules when they feel they must, but as one said, "We should not have to circumvent the system, doing 'wrong' in order to do 'right.'" Another remarked, "The bean counters have too much power." The problem is, who has the responsibility? The principal. Who has the authority? Someone else. This is a recipe for poor service to our children.

Under decentralization, it is possible to be much more responsive to student needs. Flexibility was the most resounding result of my 7-year study. For better or worse, flexibility is virtually guaranteed. By allowing dollars to be moved around, a remarkable degree of maneuverability is introduced (see Figure 3.2). Two principals made these observations about school-based management:

> We are now able to supply equipment like computers and the extra overhead projectors which the faculty felt they would never receive in the past.

> We placed $1000 in our professional development fund. . . . We could never do that before.

A number of writers have supported the idea that all organizations could use more flexibility. Peter Drucker (1986) calls for the reduction of rules. Peters and Waterman (1982) inspired a generation of business lead- ers with their views on increased autonomy. Others have advocated that schools and districts be debureau- cratized and that teachers be empowered. For a more

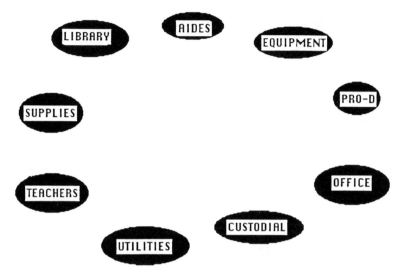

Figure 3.1. School Accounts Prior to Decentralization

NOTE: This sample of accounts shows them existing in isolation from each other. Almost no transfer is possible between any pair of accounts because the resources come as dedicated allocations.

complete look at the reasoning behind the need for flexibility, see my book *Decentralization and School-based Management* (Brown, 1990).

But once you've got it, flexibility demands planning, seen as desirable by writers such as John Goodlad in *A Place Called School* (1984), wherein he recommends, "every tub on its own bottom" and that schools should have the authority to allocate their own resources as much as possible. Teachers and principals, he notes, would like more say in school resource allocation. And he adds that planning groups within the school should deliberate so allocations may be improved.

School-based management brings ample discretion to schools. Many principals have pointed out items that they believed could never have been acquired under centralized management. In fact, flexibility was the most prominent, most widely agreed-on outcome in my extensive

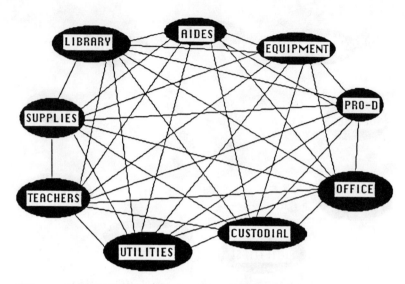

Figure 3.2. School Accounts After Decentralization

NOTE: This sample of main school accounts shows how transfers may be made between any pair. Although it is not likely that one account would be wiped out in favor of another, the flexibility exists to move funds among accounts freely after initial planning is done.

study of decentralization. But there are limits to this kind of freedom. State curricula are mandated, laws are to be obeyed, and school board policy is to be carried out. For instance, as one principal noticed, "You can't clean house and you have to live within the bounds of the union contract."

The new freedom also points to the possibility of innovations coming from schools, as Goodlad suggests. One principal noted, "Teachers know that 'if we can come up with something, we can try it out'. As a result, they are prepared to discuss more options. They are not afraid to put forward an idea which costs money." A senior administrator commented on the difference between centralization and decentralization in this way: "Formerly, it was easier to get forgiveness than permission. Now, under decentralization, it is easier to get permission than forgiveness." Although the idea that schools may show special initiatives is an inspiring one, it must be noted that research evidence is not sufficient to support this claim. The opportunity for innovation is there, but not necessarily the impetus, as initiatives are not normally rewarded with more resources.

Enhanced Accountability to the Public

At present, school personnel in centralized districts do not feel particularly accountable to anyone. And why should they? They do not shape the resources for learning. Many others besides principals and teachers have a direct say in school affairs. The multiple-boss rule applies. No wonder schools are called "loosely coupled" organizations. Confusion reigns over responsibility and authority. School personnel presumably are responsible for student learning but they do not have the authority to control school resources. Although schools are in charge of their supplies budgets, they are not normally allowed to carry them over to the next fiscal year, prompting one principal to remark that this was like "giving a child a week's allowance on Thursday and saying that if it was not spent by Saturday, it would be returned."

Under centralization, assessment on how schools are performing is often infrequent. Not only does the school board not usually know how much is spent on various programs, few indicators are normally provided to show the various levels of program success or failure. And only rarely is some statement made to show the extent to which students and parents are satisfied with the service provided them. Figure 3.3 depicts a district under centralized management. Notice that some schools take their marching orders from board members and others from persons in the central office staff. You won't see

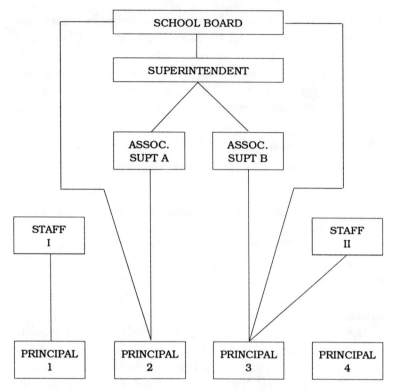

Figure 3.3. An Example of a Real-World Centralized District
            Structure

NOTE: The lines that connect the main roles in the district hierarchy show the
ability to direct as they proceed downward and accountability as they travel
upward. Notice the absence of connecting lines between some roles and the direct
lines that link other pairs. For instance:

- Principal 1 ignores her associate superintendent.
- Principal 2 has a pipeline to the board.
- Principal 3 takes orders from everybody.
- Principal 4 says he is "accountable to the kids."

those lines of influence on the district's organizational
chart, but that's exactly how many centralized districts
function.

The desire for more accountability in education was
always around. But it was given new impetus by *A Nation
at Risk.* Board members, parents, and others want to

know where the money goes and what the results are. Also, the new thrust has come from a desire to empower teachers. The Carnegie Forum (1988) and the American Federation of Teachers support this position. (See the discussion under the heading "Two Major Forms of School-Based Management" in Chapter 2.)

Let's say that your district opts for organizational decentralization, wherein schools are responsible to individual superintendents and ultimately the board. If schools are going to be given newfound freedom to spend money the way they think best, then logic requires that they be called to account for their decisions by assessments of their performance. Although valid measures of learning achievement are hard to come by, measurements are still possible on the extent to which schools are perceived as doing a good job by students, parents, and by the district employees.

Some districts that are organizationally decentralized achieve this aim by administering annual surveys of satisfaction that are broken down by school and by programs within schools. As "percentage satisfied" may be compared across schools and programs, how schools are doing can be seen by providing each with its own results as compared to district norms. One principal confessed that he and his buddies got on the phone to "compare report cards" when the results were released. Such measures may only be crude indicators of all the good things schools do, yet they certainly show what programs are perceived to be failing so that actions for improvement may be taken by school and district personnel. In my extensive study of school-based management, I found that accountability of all personnel was enhanced when districts applied such satisfaction surveys. See Figure 3.4 for a simple depiction of the structure of an organizationally decentralized district. The one-boss rule is in place; schools are accountable only to one person—their respective associate superintendent.

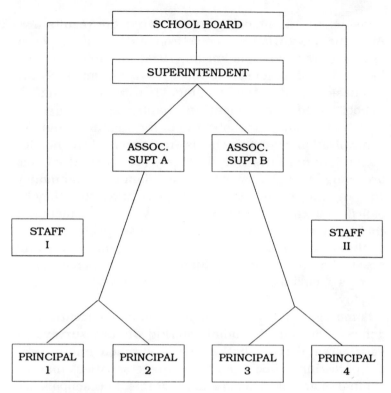

Figure 3.4. An Example of an Organizationally Decentralized
        Structure

NOTE: The ability to control the remaining district-level decisions (which flows
downward) and accountability for all decisions (which flows upward) are quite
simple to follow because the one-boss rule is applied. There are no authority/ac-
countability flows between principals and central office staffs or directly to the
school board.

If the decision is made to adopt political decentralization, then your parent or teacher council will not be
just advisory to the principal—it will make policy about
many of same matters as its counterpart for a private
school. Such independent or parochial governing boards
hire and fire their headmasters and headmistresses.
They make other personnel appointments and establish

the curricular directions for their schools. They also take responsibility for setting tuition levels and raising money for special ventures, such as additions onto school buildings.

Under parallel conditions, public school parents and teachers are given a vote in the policy directions of the school. They may plan staffing levels, employ or dismiss the principal, participate in the development of local curricula, and become involved in other important decisions affecting their school. Although considerable levels of control over curricula and funding are left to the district and the state, the influence of parents or teachers is strong. This form of school-based management is described by Marburger (1985). It is applied in Chicago where local school councils consist of the principal, six elected parents, two elected community residents, and two elected teachers. The councils in Chicago determine the reappointment of the principal and, most important, approve the school budget. The board, however, retains some powers over the councils. For a full account of the remarkable story of Chicago's experience with decentralization, see *School Restructuring: Chicago Style* (1991) by Fred Hess, an active participant in the reform there.

The politically decentralized form is also applicable to many British local educational authorities, who are now adopting school-based management. School governing boards in Britain have elected parent representatives, local councilors, an elected teacher's representative, plus others who may be invited to serve. These boards are responsible for the appointment of the head teacher. Schools with an enrollment of over 200 manage their own budget. Parts of Australia also sport their version of political decentralization, described by Brian Caldwell and Jim Spinks in their book titled *The Self-Managing School* (1988). Although composition of the school council

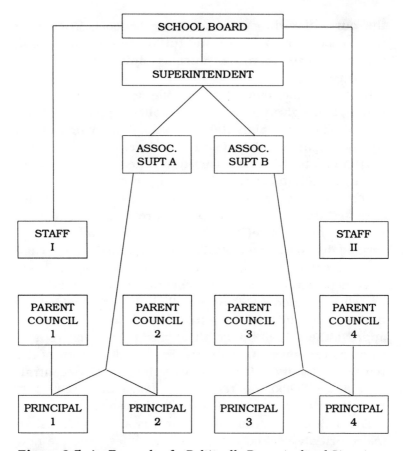

Figure 3.5. An Example of a Politically Decentralized Structure

NOTE: Although this structure is quite similar to that depicted in Figure 3.4, here the parent groups are given considerable control over the schools. The one-boss rule is varied, with some decisions made by the parents and others by the school board.

and its responsibilities vary, the emphasis is clearly on planning and the control of schools. See Figure 3.5 for a simple illustration of a district that is decentralized politically. Observe that the one-boss rule is varied to accommodate the local council.

Greater School Productivity

Are schools in decentralized districts more productive? As one principal whom I interviewed said, "If you walk down the halls of schools with and without school-based management, you won't see any difference." He is probably right, yet the small amount of research on decentralized districts and on school effectiveness in general suggests that school-based management has some potential to increase the level of service to children. Does it save money? It is not likely to save dollars because the cost per pupil tends to remain the same. Schools will spend almost all the money they are given. The small savings realized in one corner of the budget will be dispensed in another.

When asked about their spending habits under centralized conditions, curiously enough, educators are quick to mention problems that seem more akin to Eastern Europe under communism than to North American schools. They admitted to budget padding so that they could receive what was essential. They hoarded supplies, sometimes several years' worth, just to have enough. They typically had an oversupply of what was not needed from central office and an undersupply of what was needed, whether it was supplies, equipment, or personnel. One principal wanted a social worker rather than a reading specialist because his kids needed the former. No way.

Worse, to those who think schools are treated fairly by central offices, goodies were given to schools under the arrangement of "squeaky-wheel budgeting." This means that principals who belonged to the old boys' club or those who were just good at whining and cultivating relations with influentials downtown could get many more resources for their schools. A former principal in Cleveland

34 EXPLORATION

observed, "People knew me and knew that I was principal of the school where the daughter of the board presi-
dent was enrolled. . . . There were other principals who
could get nothing." In my study of school-based management, principals in decentralized districts agreed
that they would not want to return to squeaky-wheel
budgeting.

Principals in districts with school-based management
often remark on how the school is more able to match the
resources to the children's needs. Some think that more
faculty are required: "We conserve supplies and take
better care of the building in order to divert money into
the teaching personnel account." Others say that they can
do a variety of things to improve their schools, such as
"update the library with its 50-year-old books on Africa"
or "send teachers and aides to conferences, workshops
and inservice training" or "have artists in residence for
brief periods" or "allow two field trips per student per
year." Such things are possible and, it seems, desirable.
One principal in Cleveland put the idea emphatically: "If
teachers don't have the resources to teach, how are they
going to get the job done?"

But is such a decentralized arrangement fair? Clearly,
resources are likely to be consumed rather unequally
across schools. Note how the resources are given. They
are distributed via an allocation system based mostly on
pupil counts at so many dollars per pupil. These resources arrive as a lump sum and are not influenced as
much by squeaky wheels—principals who lobby for ex-
tras. So equality of access has been strengthened. But
students are treated differently depending on their requirements as perceived by the school. When pupils need
library books they get them. When the children need
sports equipment, it is forthcoming. When a learning
assistance teacher is required, one is found.

Readers familiar with the current literature on school
effectiveness and school improvement will recognize some

strong parallels between school-based management and these two themes. The start of school effectiveness movement is largely attributed to the work of Edmonds (1979). This line of research, summarized by Purkey and Simit (1983), suggests that decentralization with strong instructional leadership, collaborative planning with teachers, and the specification of common goals would lead to increased achievement. The movement toward school improvement, propelled significantly by research done by Huberman and Crandall (1982), stressed the need to involve teachers in decision making and the importance of the principal's leadership. For a more detailed account of the relationship between school-based management, school effectiveness, and school improvement, see my book on decentralization (Brown, 1990).

It is not hard to argue that the greater flexibility and accountability provided by decentralization should permit schools to raise achievement levels. Actually, some districts have hitched their hopes to specific outcomes such as increases in reading or mathematics scores and reduction in dropout rates. But don't bet your professional reputation on that happening. I find such optimism heartening but worrisome. The attainment of such objectives may require more than just decentralization. I am dubious that the extremely serious problems faced by some districts can be solved by just giving more authority to schools, though "power to the school" cannot hurt. Lieberman and Miller (1990) share some of this uncertainty about reform through decentralization.

> Schools may organize in a nonbureaucratic fashion, improve the professional lives of teachers and expand their roles, challenge regulations and remove boundaries—and *still* accomplish very little of value for students. What works in school restructuring may be relative and context-specific. But what matters is absolute and universal. (p. 764)

Some persons believe that schools will seize the opportunity to develop their own curricula. But this outcome
is uncertain because teachers are much more concerned
with instruction and they tend to accept those curricula
suggested by the district or state. The possibility of instructional changes may be more promising insofar as
planning and resources can make a difference.

What's more, decentralization is not all roses. One of
the recurring complaints among educators in decentralized districts is that the planning process is highly time-
consuming, particularly for principals and teachers in
their first year of school-based management. In fact, as
those who have tried it will tell you, the new tasks create stress. It is difficult to say if these problems reduce
their productivity as some of their time would otherwise
be spent on pursuits directed toward student learning.
However, it may be that planning for resource allocation is a very good investment that pays off in student
achievement.

One hopeful relief from some of the burden of overwork
is the automation of budgets and accounts thanks to
school-based microcomputers. Along with bookkeepers in
large schools, they can reduce the drudgery of dealing
with figures. The fact that computer-automated budgeting and accounting can be managed fairly easily permits
principals to tend to their leadership roles rather than
getting bogged down as technicians. One principal under
school-based management shared his attitude this way:
"I have trouble booting a unit up. I don't want to spend
my time this way; I want to work with people. I can have
others generate the printouts."

Although it is fine to say that resources are matched
to student needs, is there any other evidence that school
productivity might be increased? If productivity may
be equated with parental and student satisfaction with
schools, some evidence from my study on school-based
management suggests that it may be increased when a

district decentralizes. Based on the annual surveys in Edmonton during the period before and after restructuring, the following overall pattern was evident: U.S. schools were going down in parental satisfaction, Canadian schools remained the same, yet satisfaction with Edmonton schools was going up. No mean feat.

4 Strategic Decisions at the Exploration Stage

Main sources of opposition to district decentralization are of two kinds. One comes from legitimate ideas that are incompatible with the beliefs behind school-based management. This guidebook presents them in the section entitled "Why *Not* Decentralize?" and you are encouraged to judge them for their own strengths and weaknesses. However, the other source is from motives that most persons would consider shady, manipulative, or self-serving. Often these impulses stem from a desire to maintain power, influence, and control over resources that might be redistributed through decentralization. Who might oppose school-based management with these motives, which only their cronies would support? How might these power-mongers try to neutralize or kill the idea of decentralization? Attributing motives to others is risky — one can misinterpret others actions easily; but with that caveat, here are some examples.

Subversion and Suspects

Some Persons Inside the Board Office

Some board members or central office employees may see decentralization as a threat to their power base and the resources they control. A board member who is not interested in policy matters but wants to make rules for schools may cultivate other board members' fears that they will no longer be able to affect individual schools with their private agendas. Then he or she may vote to allocate only a small percentage of total district resources for schools to manage with no hope of further increases. Later, this board member will help make the introduction to school-based management so protracted that your district can never really get around to it.

Not wanting to give up the authority to manage schools directly, leadership for decentralization may not be delegated to a lieutenant. In that manner, the idea will be nobody's baby and die of neglect. So that disillusionment will be sure to follow, he or she will cultivate the expectation that decentralization will cure most problems facing schools. He or she will be certain to exhibit no courage or trust in your school personnel. In effect, the strategy will be to provide no moral support for the idea of decentralization. Or, to ensure that your district adopts decentralization in name only, this member will make sure that all his or her schools have supplies budgets already and, hence, school-based management. The fact that every other district in the country is decentralized by this definition will escape some onlookers. Another strategy, almost as cunning, is, first, to forget the idea. When that fails, oppose with moral persuasion. When that doesn't work, adopt superficially.

As another example, think of an assistant superintendent who wants to retain control of an empire of personnel and its budget. She may convince the school board that principals and teachers are financially incompetent because they have never been allowed to handle substantial amounts of money before. She will stress the point that they are just not trainable in the complexities of finance. The fact that she was once a teacher herself and subsequently trained in financial matters will be overlooked.

As a coordinator or supervisor whose influence will lessen and who may have to return to a teaching job, an opponent may cast aspersions on the trustworthiness of school personnel with regard to student welfare, citing extreme cases that have been dredged up elsewhere.

Some Persons Outside the District Structure

Some union or parental activists may regard school-based management as a threat to their ability to influence or control schools.

A teacher's union representative may be afraid of loss of union ability to set rules for schools via contracts. So, he may hire an "expert" known to be hostile to the idea to visit the district and to tell stories of disasters and failures with decentralization. Thus the idea is condemned, rather than specific methods of implementation that were bungled in other districts.

A support staff union representative who may lose influence could circulate rumors of support staff layoffs that might result from the decisions principals make. That this outcome is unlikely will not reduce its ability to magnify anxiety among the members.

A parent who wants to continue to have a direct, personal influence on schools could attack the idea because, in her view, schools might become more different than they are today, thus reducing equality. She might brand the idea as contrary to equal educational opportunity and help to make decentralization more of an ideological issue than a pragmatic one.

Some Persons in Schools

Not everyone in schools will favor decentralization; we know that for sure. Some will be afraid of its responsibilities or find school-based management incompatible with their inability to share decision making.

On the one hand, a weak principal, afraid of hard-nosed decision making, might try to blame central office for things that can't be done in his school. On the other hand, an influential principal who gets more than her share of the goodies via contacts with central office personnel might be sure to assert that her school runs just fine without decentralization.

Consider an autocratic principal who is fearful of the requirement to consult with faculty, or a principal who would like to avoid working with teachers on important decisions about school programs. These administrators might insist that principals have ample power now and that school-based management would produce undue faculty or parental influence over decision-making.

Why Not Decentralize?

Districts are ill advised to proceed with decentralization in certain times and circumstances:

- when other major initiatives are under way;
- when the district is experiencing severe retrenchment;
- when the district is quite small; and
- when there is major disagreement in principle.

Although many excuses may be given for why a district may not want to move to school-based management, it must be remembered that a good number of reasons are valid, too. Here are the four important ones.

First, if the district is currently undertaking major initiatives on its own or at state request, such as sizable curricular changes, personnel will be burdened with the job of implementing them. Only so many changes can be properly addressed at any one time, as the job of delivering normal service is quite demanding for most educators. As is shown in the following chapters, restructuring with decentralization is a sizable change that requires ample attention.

Another good reason for not proceeding to decentralize is the advent of retrenchment. When states cut back money for districts and they in turn must release personnel, the level of preoccupation with the cutbacks is most distracting; most people feel threatened even if their jobs are not in direct jeopardy. At that time, they tend to confuse the move to school-based management with retrenchment itself, believing that its purpose is to reduce faculty and staff. This confusion tends to poison the implementation effort. In Broward County, Florida, the board decided to handle the cutbacks centrally, a policy that led the district to abandon school-based management. In my study, people in districts that changed to school-based management during a period of funding cutbacks said it was a very bad time to decentralize.

A third valid reason for not decentralizing is small size. Districts with small enrollments (let's say less than 1,000 pupils) have the advantage of close connections between their schools and their central offices. Although some have decentralized and feel they have benefited, others do not see the need when school personnel work directly with central office to determine school resources. The idea just makes less sense for them. Naturally, the same argument may be applied in reverse; large districts may have the most to gain from school-based management.

You will notice that the first three reasons are solid, pragmatic ones. Yet there is another kind of reason why you might not follow this trend. The fourth reason is one of principle and raises more fundamental issues about the directions your school district may wish to take. It is possible to disagree honestly with the reasons for decentralization, and persons who do so should be given the opportunity to speak their views. No policy change is without arguments for and against it, and it is important that both sides be considered. Let's contemplate the down side of school-based management.

One very good reason for not decentralizing is that it is not seen as desirable. What is it that your district really wants to do? Is decentralization necessary to achieve those objectives? If your school personnel believe they have sufficient flexibility to make the decisions they want to make, if the parents in your district already support their schools strongly, and if it is not clear how school productivity may be increased because of decentralization, then why do it? The pressures to be trendy may overwhelm the sober thought required to make such a long-term decision. Carl Glickman (1990), a leading observer of restructuring, warns,

> Having worked closely for many years with schools engaged in [school empowerment, decentralization of educational decision making, school-based staff development, and site-based management], I'm wary of schoolpeople's impulse to jump on the restructuring bandwagon without assessing their own readiness to take on the pain and to confront the conflicts involved—and without realizing the extraordinary courage necessary to sustain such change. (p. 68)

He adds,

> If schools move too quickly and without a clear picture of the issues at stake, they will fail to improve education for

students. And legislators will perceive that failure as another example of why teachers and schools need to be
controlled and monitored more strictly than ever. With decentralization, the stakes are high. Education as a profession has much to gain, but it also has much to lose. (p. 69)

Another red flag comes from Larry Cuban (1990), a
professor at Stanford University, who sees reforms such
as decentralization as just cyclical; each is a bandwagon
to be abandoned within a few years. In fact, Mintzberg
(1983) even argues that decentralization in all organizations is unstable and likely to revert to a centralized
structure. Other experts have expressed similar reserva-
tions. One reason for a return to centralization would be
because schools are perceived to be insufficiently accountable to the public they serve.

Further, a major preparation effort as well as a high
level of commitment to the idea are both required. If the
weight of the argument is in favor of *not* decentralizing
because a change to school-based management is seen as
wrong, then no "critical mass" for change and no general
acceptance of the idea will exist. Under such conditions,
it probably should not proceed because the implementation effort itself will fail (more on the change to school-
based management in later chapters).

Appointment of a Champion

One way that decentralization can be given a considerable boost in your district is through the appointment of
a champion. Such a person, often given the title of direc-
tor of school-based management, is the one who shoul-
ders considerable responsibility for the exploration of
the idea. This key figure, usually a high-ranking central
office employee, will gain the initial knowledge about
the beliefs and aims of decentralization. He or she will

gather information, attend conferences, and visit decentralized districts to get the initial facts. This person could assemble an introductory workshop using experts and materials gathered. Options need to be laid out. As one superintendent said, "You have got to have somebody who is the keeper of the vision." If such a person is not appointed, it is quite likely that no one will take responsibility for decentralization and the idea will die a "natural" death.

End of the Exploration Stage

The exploration stage has mainly been concerned with collecting information about school-based management. Once armed with that information, your district has ensured wide discussion of the idea, appointed one person responsible for the thrust of decentralization, and stood on guard against subversive actions. Now, let's assume that the school board has examined the evidence and heard the discussion. It then decides to be courageous and votes to put the idea "on trial." You're gutsy. Now what? As shown in the next chapter, much work is still to be done.

STAGE II

TRIAL

So the decision has been made to try school-based management for a selected set of schools, and it is hoped that the experience will be a positive one—a way of adapting to the changing conditions faced by your schools. However, probably more failures have been caused by bungled start-ups than by application of the innovation to the wrong setting or at the wrong time. That is why the trial stage must be managed with great care and sufficient resources. A whole lot of hard work lies ahead. If school-based management is introduced the wrong way or for the wrong reasons, watch out: Failure is very likely.

One way decentralization can be a flop is by its adoption in a wholesale, unthinking way. If another district's version is completely copied onto your local setting, quite likely many aspects will not fit because the model must be adapted. In fact, planning should be undertaken so that those most affected contribute their ideas to make it work, thus deriving a sense of ownership from their inputs. This suggestion of local initiative leads me to believe that voluntary adoption by a district has a greater chance of success than a mandated one, particularly statewide. Florida's lack of implementation in the mid-1970s bears this out. If districts can contemplate and implement the idea at their own pace, the prospect of recentralization should be lessened. Remarkably, successful implementation can occur even when decentralization is required by some external authority such as a court or state legislature.

Succinctly, the trial stage involves these challenges:

• development of policy statements that show the aims and principles of decentralization, along with its form (organizational or political) and scope (what decisions will be decentralized initially);
• efforts to maximize the information about school-based management among all personnel and an involvement of all stakeholders in key decisions about decentralization;
• work on an initial method that is to be used to allocate dollars to schools, mostly on a per-student basis;
• construction of a process of district and school planning involving budgets, and specification of roles and dates;
• work on how schools are to be held accountable for their decisions, by surveys of satisfaction or other means;
• initiation of the pilot school program, probably involving six schools of varying kinds and lasting 2 years;
• facilitation of the many role changes on the part of board members, central office staff, principals, teachers, support staff, and parents; and
• defense against acts of sabotage on the part of those who, often for personal reasons, want the experiment to be shelved.

5 Development of District Policy

As the district moves from horizontal decentralization (where authority is shared with central office staff) to vertical decentralization (where authority is shared with schools), many questions loom as to how this shift will be done.

The most fundamental issue to resolve at this stage is whether parents or teachers will be given a mandate over schools using parental councils, or if the district school board will retain control of schools through its administrators. As discussed on pages 30-32, parental or teacher control of schools implies that school council authority and its limits must be clearly established. The demarcation between the authority of the school council and that of the district school board also needs to be delineated. However, if "ultimate" authority is to be retained in the school board, a clear division is needed between those central office persons in that line of authority and those who are in staff positions.

The next basic issue to be faced in the scope of decentralization, as outlined on pages 18-21. Just what

decisions are to be decentralized? Basically, two choices
are evident at this stage.

One is to permit school allocations to include equipment and supplies only. Such a change may seem small
but it will come as a shock to schools that have had
virtually no freedom to switch dollars between accounts
before. This alternative permits districts to become familiar with decentralization slowly, providing a pace they
may value. This experience can provide the groundwork
for an increase in scope to include faculty and support
personnel later. Such a modest start, however, also presents the danger that the district may never "get there," as
a protracted implementation time may permit distrac-
tions to arise and opposition to muster.

The other alternative is to include—right from the
start—equipment, supplies, faculty, and support staff
among the decisions to decentralize. They represent the
bulk of a school's resources and can amount to 85% of
district operating budgets. Such a choice demands more
pluck and more preparation. Although this allows the
change to school-based management to be accomplished
sooner, it also increases the impact of mistakes in planning. Notice that the inclusion of central office services
is not suggested at this stage in decentralization. For
those who want to do something about "the blob," such
a strategy may be disappointing. It is probably wiser,
however, to try to decentralize the decisions that require a smaller and simpler cope of authority rather than
the entire spectrum of possibilities at once. And some
decisions should probably always remain at the board
office. Greenhalgh (1984), a former school superintendent who has written about school-based management,
recommends that a number of specific functions be retained at the central office. They include those listed in
Table 5.1. Those topics covered in collective agreements
are also possibilities for decentralization. Consequently,

TABLE 5.1
Central Costs That Schools Probably Should Not Bear

---

  (1) attendance service
  (2) bulk supplies purchases
  (3) business services
  (4) census and pupil enumeration
  (5) continuing education
  (6) core central administration costs
  (7) data processing
  (8) district-initiated program start-ups
  (9) dues collection
(10) fees and memberships
(11) payroll
(12) personnel relations
(13) personnel services
(14) research costs
(15) retirement incentives
(16) testing expenses
(17) transportation (daily)

SOURCE: Adapted from Greenhalgh (1984, pp. 58-59, 81).

unions may worry that their bargaining may be reduced
to the school site. One offered as a guideline:

> That all matters related to salary, benefits, working condi-
> tions, personnel practice and tenure be subject to nego-
> tiations between the board and appropriate employee
> unions, and be *ultra vire* [beyond the purview of] school-
> based decision-making.

If such decisions were placed at the school level they
would bring major changes well beyond those created
from the move to decentralization as normally conceived.
Unless your district wants to experiment in labor-
management relations, prudence dictates that the usual
contract provisions be maintained and honored when
agreements are signed.

52

TRIAL

TABLE 5.2
Sample Goals for School District Decentralization

---

(1) To provide principals and teachers with an appropriate and effective role in the decision-making process in education

(2) To provide a decision-making mechanism that is responsive to the needs of students

(3) To develop a valid system of accountability

(4) To ensure the effectiveness of the expenditure of the educational dollar

(5) To give the budget/planning process a direct educational focus

---

SOURCE: From the School District of Langley, British Columbia

Once these hard decisions have been made, it is important for districts to develop policy statements regarding decentralization. As is shown in Table 5.2, they may take the form of goals for school-based management.

Another form of policy statement found helpful is one that accentuates the principles of school-based management or prohibits the breakage of those principles. Some examples are shown in Table 5.3.

Information and Involvement

Districts that have adopted school-based management successfully have tended to maximize the amount of information about decentralization. At the same time, those districts involved all those persons in and associated with the district who were to be affected by the change. Those people included virtually everybody who had any interest in how administrative decisions were made. Among the more obvious groups were board members, central office staff, principals, teachers, support staff, parents, and senior students. There are many avenues available for conveying information and promoting discussion, such as professional development sessions,

TABLE 5.3
Sample Principles Associated With
School District Decentralization

Each individual shall have only one supervisor.

No one shall have authority to direct or veto any decision or action where that person is not accountable for the results.

The organization should avoid uniform rules, practices, policies, and regulations that are designed to protect the organization against "mistakes."

Concentration on administrative concerns is designed to significantly improve the framework within which we work so that people can concentrate their energies on addressing educational concerns, not dissipate their energies overcoming administrative friction and obstacles.

Headquarters is prohibited from deciding on those topics delegated to cluster* directors and to principals. Cluster directors and principals must themselves decide what to do.

SOURCE: Cleveland Public Schools, Edmonton Public Schools.
*Clusters are groups of schools under one associate superintendent.

workshops, meetings, breakfasts, and informal gatherings, even teas. One of the reasons why decentralization fails is the lack of information about it. Efforts to get the word out and permit open discussion could not be more important.

Some groups tend to agree with the ideas behind decentralization less readily than do others. Unions and other stakeholders should be approached in an open and honest manner. If they feel that the district's ulterior aim for decentralization is to reduce the number of positions, then they will rightfully oppose the idea. Remember, too, that unions serve to protect their members from capricious principals and, for them, decentralization may mean giving too much power to principals. After all, part of the reason for their existence is to give their membership a measure of security. Such protection often comes in the form of rules that each school is required to obey, such as the number of counselors required per pupil. Although such rules protect jobs and the people in them, the difficulty is that they present the same kind of inflexibilities that precise rules from the board do. Their rules get in the way of the school's ability to supply the kinds of resources to the tasks needed for student learning. Is there a way to reconcile concerns about security with the need for flexibility?

The manner in which decentralized districts have tackled the problem of security with flexibility is ensure that union contracts and their rules are upheld. Personnel are sometimes allocated according to ratios, such as 1 teacher to 25 students. However, schools are permitted to vary from the numbers allocated. The result is that through contract waivers, schools do not always end up with that exact ratio, but deviate from it. If unions know that their own membership will be involved in decisions that result in variations from the contract, then they find it easier to agree with the outcomes at the school level. Such arrangements reduce the "we/they" division that often exists between teachers and their employers. As one principal observed, "There is a power shift to teachers in the school."

6 Development of the Allocation Method

Decentralization requires that an allocation formula be constructed. This formula gives resources to schools so that they can educate the students under their care for 1 year. Remember that it is not a set of fixed resources. Rather it is a lump-sum amount to be varied (within limits) by the school — a box of silver dollars.

Most of the money allotted to schools is given according to the rule "The dollar follows the child" (see Figure 6.1). An amount is allocated, usually in the range of $2,000 to $4,000 per typical child when teacher resources are included. (For an example of an allocation system that is school enrollment driven, see Table 6.1.) The remaining money can be apportioned by taking into consideration such matters as particular programs, multiple programs, new school start-up costs, building maintenance, transiency, enrollment changes, and school size. School size presents a special problem. Thanks to the financial notion of "economy of scale," there is an advantage accredited to large size as far as discretionary spending is

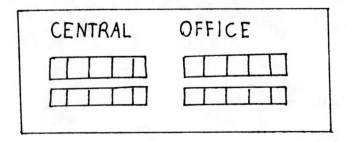

L. J. B.

Figure 6.1. The Dollar Follows the Child

TABLE 6.1
An Indicative Resource Allocation System

Category of Student	Number of FTEs	Allocation Rate (in dollars)
Kindergarten	425	2,600
Elementary (1-6)	2,913	2,600
Junior high (7-9)	1,517	2,700
Senior high (10-12)	1,359	2,750
Senior vocational/technical	1,102	3,300
English as a second language (1-12)	457	3,600
Trades and service	164	4,200
Learning disabled	42	7,200
Trainable mentally handicapped	18	8,200
Behavior disordered	25	12,100
Dependent handicapped	16	12,100
Autistic	8	18,000
Blind	6	18,000

concerned. Small schools have very little left over after they have spent their basic allocation, so the linear scale is varied in some way. For instance, one district's formula allows $95,000 for a school with no students(!), which decreases gradually to provide no extra dollars for schools with an enrollment larger than 300 students.

What do allocations look like for individual schools? See Table 6.2 for sample allocation forecasts across three schools. Although allocations "try" to be fair by giving roughly the same amount per pupil, not all are handed out in that way. Disbursements "try" to be fair by being varied to accommodate particular programs and circumstances, such as disability and transiency.

As just assumed, teachers and other professional resources may be allocated by amounts per pupil. Another way to divvy up the pot is to allocate one teacher per number of children, say 25. As long as the teacher is given

TABLE 6.2
Three Allocation Forecasts

AN ELEMENTARY SCHOOL

Number of Students	Allocation Category	Rate	Dollar Allocation
26	Kindergarten	2,600	67,600
196	Regular	2,600	509,600
22	English as a second language	3,600	79,200
4	Autistic	18,000	72,000
21	Dependent handicapped	12,100	254,100
	Community use		1,900
	Transiency		8,900
269	TOTAL		993,300

A JUNIOR SECONDARY SCHOOL

Number of Students	Allocation Category	Rate	Dollar Allocation
534	Regular	2,700	1,441,800
6	Behavior disordered	12,100	72,600
1	Blind	12,100	123,000
15	Trainable mentally handicapped	8,200	12,100
	Special program		31,500
	Computer grant		5,500
	Transiency		12,600
556	TOTAL		1,699,100

A SENIOR SECONDARY SCHOOL

Number of Students	Allocation Category	Rate	Dollar Allocation
900	Regular	2,750	2,475,000
400	Vocational/technical	3,300	1,320,000
95	English as second language	3,800	361,000
10	Learning disabled	7,200	72,000
350	Trades and services	4,200	1,470,000
	Transiency		38,000
1,755	TOTAL		5,736,000

a dollar equivalent, then the school receives the person but can swap the teacher for other items (or other items for the teacher—both exchanges are okay). Regardless of how teachers and other professionals are allocated, decentralized districts have tended to fix the price of a teacher at the average district teacher salary. That way, the experience of any teacher (and thus his or her actual salary) is not related to any financial decisions made under decentralization. This point is vital, so permit me to restate: Experienced and inexperienced teachers cost the same to the school and so the school's decision concerning the number of teachers it wants is not affected by the actual experience level of teachers in the building. Such an arrangement completely eliminates the possibility that a principal could recruit a faculty of inexperienced teachers just to save money. Teachers are acquired for their skill and not because of their salary. This problem does raise the question, though, as to why teacher pay and responsibility are usually unrelated, but that is a matter beyond decentralization.

Many particular questions are to be addressed when building an allocation system, such as how to handle sick leave, telephones, maintenance, and utilities. Each needs to be worked out clearly. Is every school resource to be included in the lump-sum allocation? No. Special education funding, as well as other categorical funding from the federal government, are examples of dollar flows that are usually (but not always) kept outside the box of silver dollars. The other exclusions include all those decisions that are not currently within the purview of the schools but could be in the future. These are usually central office services, such as consultant time.

Is such an allocation system easy to build and implement? Relatively. It can be generated on a microcomputer spreadsheet in 2 days. Such a product would be in rather rough form, but if the formula receives principal input from the first year onward, it is much more likely to gain acceptance by schools than if an elaborate set of equations is constructed at the start and then imposed. At least one point of caution is urged. It would be easy to devise an allocation system that starves some schools and stuffs others. A formula-driven allocation outcome may have little resemblance to the resources that schools are receiving today. Remember, then, that formulas are designed to be fair, but squeaky-wheel budgeting is probably not. That means that some schools are currently fat and others are lean. In order to avoid major disruptions in school staffing, it will be necessary to "reflect reality for the first year." This phrase means that the current staffing levels in each school must not be altered much until subsequent years of school-based management.

The development of an allocation mechanism is partly a matter of trial and error. One way to work on the recurrent problems of allocation is to establish a standing committee on school-based management. Such a committee is usually composed of principals, allocate superintendents, and business officers. Its job is to adapt the allocation formulas to changing conditions that could be new schools or additions to the scope of decentralization. Be assured that the membership will be most alert to the aim of equitable distribution of dollars. Besides improving the allocations, the committee's work tends to reduce complaints about the formulas that determine the "life blood" of schools.

7 Development of the Budgeting Process

For better or worse, planning for resource expenditure is a dual process. The district and the schools follow interlocking steps. The overall district operating budget is determined in conjunction with district goals for the school year, meaning from July to June. Because most districts operate on a calendar year or fiscal year, it makes sense to convert school budgeting to a school-year basis sometime later. After central costs are determined, school lump-sum allocations are approximated and schools are asked to engage in their annual planning. Actually, school planning starts earlier, but it culminates in a school budget.

For any organization, a budget is really just a financial plan. Ideally, budgets should consist of two main elements: what a school wants to do and how many dollars are required to do it. Such plans and their accompanying resource needs are broken down in detail so that agreement on the part of school personnel can be reached. Budgets are offered for approval or discussion, usually to the school's associate superintendent or a board sub-committee or both, who may impose a rule of variance of 10%. This means that schools must account clearly for a shift in planned expenditures beyond that threshold. At this point, be sure to note that the budgets do not contain just the usual line items, but also goals and objectives. In this way, board members can link what schools intend to spend with what they plan to do.

Here is an example from Edmonton. After school budgets are approved in May and an enrollment count is taken on September 30, schools receive a final allocation (the box of silver dollars—see Figure 7.1). They are required to operate within this lump sum, unless there is a surplus from the previous year. Naturally, accounting systems keep track of expenditures, usually by the month, to let schools know the rate at which their funds are expended and also to ensure that their disbursements are within the law. An example of this overall process is shown in Table 7.1 for a moderately sized suburban district.

School personnel and others will find a handbook a useful guide through the budgeting process. Manuals for district and school planning are designed to inform administrators and others just how the general budgeting process works. Here is an outline: It might be a good idea to start with the goals of your district, principles of decentralization, and aims for the current year. Then it is important to include the planning timetable, with key dates and the persons responsible. Next, people need to be informed about how allocations are determined so they can estimate their own school's expected receipts. They also need to know the costs that may be charged to them for each kind of personnel. Armed with sufficient information, they then require direction on the format their budget is expected to take. When fully laid out in useful detail, such a manual can grow to 100 pages.

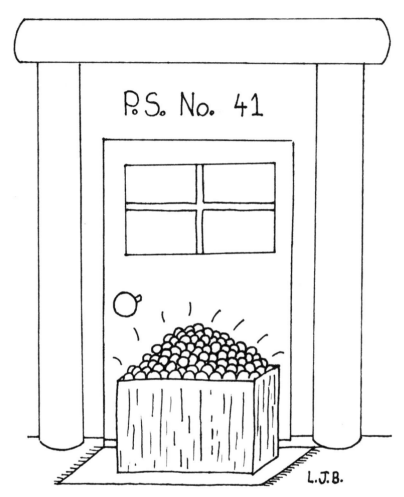

Figure 7.1. The Box of Silver Dollars

A table of contents of a sample handbook is illustrated in Table 7.2.

One important inclusion in those planning/budgeting manuals is the set of prices that schools are required to pay for services. Such prices cover all professional and support personnel. Each person's services are fixed at the

64   TRIAL

TABLE 7.1
Decentralized Suburban District Planning Schedule:
Goal Setting, Budget Planning Process

Task	Completion Date
Allocation formulae revision	February 28
Head teacher inservice	February 21
Principal inservice—basic review of allocation manual and organizational operation	
Preliminary resource allocation to schools	March 13-15
Parent survey submitted to assistant superintendent	March 26
Results of parent survey to schools	March 30-April 4
Goal-setting day	April 9
Second enrollment forecast to be sent to schools	April 16
Enrollment verification by principals	April 27
Revised resource allocation to schools	May 2
School goals/budget submitted to assistant superintendent for reaction and approval	May 14
School goals/budget submitted to superintendent	
Trustee School Plan Review Committee	May 23
School goals/budget to be approved by board	May 25
Verify enrollments and allocate accordingly	June 4
Revised budget (as per September 30 allocation) submitted to assistant superintendents	September 30 October 12

SOURCE: From the School District of Langley, British Columbia

average district salary rate, as indicated in Table 7.3. Another useful inclusion simply tells where to find local information (that is, whom to call). See Table 7.4 for a sample.

As indicated, in this "new day" of governance, schools specify their own priorities, link other priorities with district goals, indicate how objectives will be achieved, and submit their budgets. The details of school planning are beyond the scope of this guidebook but general plans are outlined in template form in Table 7.5. Actual plans from the Edmonton Public Schools show a number of

TABLE 7.2
Suburban District Budgeting Manual Contents

SOURCE: From the School District of Langley, British Columbia.

TABLE 7.3
Examples of Unit Costs Charged to Schools

Category of Personnel	Unit Cost (in dollars)
Professional	
Teachers, counselors	41,200
Principal	41,200 + 10%
Assistant principal	41,200 + 5%
Department head	41,200 + 3,500
Support staff	
Grade 2	15,000
Grade 4	20,000
Grade 6	27,000
Grade 8	33,000
Grade 10	44,000
Custodial	
Head Custodian	
up to 100,000 square feet	23,000
over 100,000 square feet	26,000
Custodian	21,000
Assistant	16,000
Hourly employees	Actual plus benefits

interesting patterns: School priorities reflect district priorities; indicators or results are specified; school priorities for the year are laid out in some detail; actions are
offered with dates and responsibilities; line item budgets
are appended. Priorities and actions vary in detail from
school to school. My impression is that the willingness
to participate in this kind of planning may differ across
schools. Although these plans represent a step toward
program budgeting, wherein achieved results are matched
to actual costs incurred, they fall short of that objective.
Rather, the plans indicate priorities and costs for the
school in general (which is a lot more specific than for the
district as a whole).

TABLE 7.4
Whom to Call for Help in the Budgeting Manual

Whom Should I Approach for Advice/Assistance in Matters Pertaining to . . .

• Budget variance	Zonal assistant superintendent
• Employee salary agreements, personnel	Personnel officer
• Developing school goals and objectives	Assistant superintendents
• Purchasing, pricing	Supervisor of purchasing
• Resource allocation	Director of instruction
• Monitoring a school program	Assistant superintendents
• Custodial services	Custodial supervisor
• Enrollments	Director of instruction
• Curricular content	Supervisors—elective, core, special services
• The monthly financial statements, accounting	Manager of business services
• Testing	Assistant superintendent of curriculum
• Improvement of instruction	Helping teacher for effective instruction
• Buildings, grounds	Supervisor of maintenance
• Policy and legal interpretations	Secretary treasurer

SOURCE: From the School District of Langley, British Columbia.

An important element in the development of the budgeting process is the need to train participating personnel in their new roles that involve planning how money will be spent. Board members, central office personnel, principals, teachers, support staff, and parent/teacher

TABLE 7.5
A School Budget Template

PLAN [1-2 Pages]

    District Priority for Year:
    School Priorities for Year:
    Results Expected:
    Indicators of Achievement of Results:
    Schedule for Review:

ACTIONS [1-2 pages]

Description	Completion Dates	Whose Responsibility

GRID [1 page]

Resources:	Professional Salaries	Support Salaries	Other

Programs:

(Instructional, Noninstructional, in some detail)	[Where programs and resources cross, dollar allocations are shown.]

Totals in margins.

councils are involved. When the decentralization is organizational, principals need to know how to consult with teachers and support staff in order to engage them meaningfully in planning. When the decentralization is political, the parent/teacher governing council needs to know what its role is and to what extent consultation with others is required.

8 Development of the Accountability System

Although districts may be decentralized without a system to monitor school performance, a mechanism that permits schools to be compared on reasonably valid indicators provides a counterpoint for their new freedom. Schools can be evaluated in any number of ways; some decentralized districts have elected to set up a pattern of annual questionnaires that measure the levels of satisfaction registered by parents, students, and employees. Parents and students are seen as the main beneficiaries of the efforts of schools to educate children, so feedback from students and parents is critical. Employees are included because they have a great deal of specialized and inside knowledge about the workings of the district and schools.

Most survey questions are school specific and program specific. When percentages of respondents who are highly or fairly satisfied are calculated, then satisfactions with role and program performance can be matched in place and in time. In one decentralized district, a great many gradual improvements over successive years were registered on a wide variety of programs. Principals whose ratings were low on certain measures had the opportunity to address them. Assessment of school or program performance can also be used to evaluate the personnel most responsible. Because decentralization gives principals the authority to make resource deployments, it seems only fair that such survey information be used as part of their personnel evaluations. See Tables 8.1, 8.2, and 8.3 for sample questions and topics asked of parents, students, and district employees, respectively. Their responses, measured as percentage satisfied, become bases for comparisons of all kinds. For example, the district range of parental attitudes regarding aspects of academic work, school organization, staff performances, services, and communication with the school may be used as a backdrop for the actual performance of a particular school. Each school then knows its relative standing. The truth can be quite illuminating and can lead to probing questions, especially when a given school is a long way from the average. Parallel results for students and employees may also be shown.

Any districtwide survey is a complicated task to carry out. It involves sampling procedures, questionnaire formats, specification of programs and roles, selection of appropriate questions for each sample, handling of nonrespondents, means of automatically tallying responses, and dissemination of results at different levels of aggregation. All these jobs require ample planning. Such preparations are at too great a level of detail to be reported here, but the central point is this: The expertise required to mount a successful monitoring mechanism is no different from any other extensive survey's requirements.

TABLE 8.1
Questions and Topics Asked of All Parents

Are you satisfied?

(1) Vocabulary/spelling/grammar
(2) Mathematics
(3) Physical education
(4) Fine arts
(5) Do you feel your child likes school?
(6) The district is using its money in a reasonable manner
(7) Are you satisfied with your child's teachers?
(8) Are you satisfied with the school principal?
(9) Are you satisfied with the board of trustees?
(10) Do you feel welcome at the school?
(11) Satisfactorily informed about your child's learning progress?
(12) Are the nonteaching employees at the school friendly?
(13) Adequate voice in school decisions that affect you
(14) Extracurricular programs offered
(15) The way attendance is handled
(16) Number of pupils in your child's classes is appropriate
(17) Cleanliness of your child's school
(18) Guidance and counseling services
(19) Library services
(20) Number of course choices open to your child (Grades 10-12)

SOURCE: Adapted from Edmonton Public Schools.

The idea of accountability encompasses much more than a survey, however. Surveys of satisfaction provide one kind of data on which to measure performance. Many other yardsticks may be used, such as school accreditation, standardized testing, and personnel evaluations. For example, a set of school indicators is provided in Table 8.4. Also, the budgetary system of decentralization is part of the accountability effort. When budgets are subject to review and control such that board members know what dollars are spent on what programs, accountability is served. If the form of school-based management

72

TRIAL

TABLE 8.2
Sample Questions and Topics
Asked of Students of Varying Grades

Are you satisfied?

(1) Do you like your teacher?
(2) Do you like the principal?
(3) Emphasis on basic skills
(4) The extracurricular program
(5) Usefulness of your courses
(6) How much you are learning
(7) Say you have in decisions that affect you
(8) The assistant principal
(9) The office staff
(10) The way student discipline is handled
(11) School rules and regulations
(12) School buildings, grounds, and equipment
(13) The interest your teachers have in you
(14) Your homework assignments
(15) How your marks in the courses are determined
(16) Help in planning your high school program
(17) Career planning assistance
(18) Behavior of other students out of class
(19) How attendance problems are handled
(20) The student union or council
(21) Number of pupils in your classes

SOURCE: Adapted from Edmonton Public Schools.

is political and thus involves teacher or parental controlling councils for each school, then a greater degree of local accountability is achieved as well. Such councils will probably need some inservice training in order to understand their roles. Accountability is a notion that just will not go away.

TABLE 8.3
Questions and Topics
Asked of All District Employees

Are you satisfied?

(1) Good communication throughout the school district
(2) Good communication in your school/division
(3) Equipment, materials, and supplies provided
(4) Adequate influence over district-level decisions that affect you
(5) Adequate influence over school-/division-level decisions that affect you
(6) Support from the associate superintendent
(7) Support from your principal/supervisor
(8) Adequate recognition and appreciation for your performance
(9) Assigned work responsibilities are fair and reasonable
(10) District is compensating you fairly
(11) District is consistently implementing its goals, philosophies, and policies
(12) District's goals, philosophies, and practices are consistent with your goals and beliefs
(13) Respect and have confidence in the superintendent
(14) Respect and have confidence in central administration
(15) Respect and have confidence in your principal/supervisor
(16) Promotion procedures for staff are fair and reasonable
(17) District is a good place to work
(18) Instructional supporting services provided
(19) Noninstructional supporting services provided

SOURCE: Adapted from Edmonton Public Schools.

TABLE 8.4
School Indicators in Ratio Form

(1)	Administration/all expenditures
(2)	Consumer price index/all expenditures
(3)	Cost per student
(4)	Energy costs/all expenditures
(5)	Enrollment/all expenditures
(6)	Instructional costs/total costs
(7)	Library services/circulation volume
(8)	Maintenance costs/property value
(9)	Professional salaries/all salaries
(10)	Special education/all expenditures
(11)	Pupils/teachers
(12)	Staff costs/total costs
(13)	Utilities/all expenditures

SOURCE: Selected and adapted from Greenhalgh (1984, pp. 133-134).

9 The Pilot School Program and Major Role Changes

Once sufficient preparations have been undertaken, it will be time to select a set of schools to be the forerunners. Usually six or seven in number, these schools normally represent a cross-section of grades and will come forth voluntarily. Their principals really should be willing to try the idea in their schools. Such leaders tend to be quite knowledgeable about decentralization and will already have engaged in some internal preparations. If the job is imposed on unwilling schools, it is quite likely that the idea will not get a fair test, or the test will be about as fair as expecting gas heaters to sell well in the tropics. Alternatively, the selection of schools that are seen as "winners" is not necessary. They need not contain principals of exceptional ability or have stellar reputations. In fact, if only such schools are chosen, then the credibility of the experiment is undermined. Onlookers can say that the exceptional might be able to handle school-based management, but ordinary principals in mainstream schools could not. Decentralization needs to work for everybody, not just heroes and heroines.

The pilots are your district's trailblazers. They will make demands on the central office, particularly for information regarding accounts. Some will bog down in their paperwork during the first year, confusing decentralization with school-based accounting. Others will develop automated accounting systems of their own in order to monitor their expenditures because they do not altogether trust the information coming from central office. Some, not believing the flexibility that they have, will tend not to exercise it. Others will make unusual budgetary requests that will shock the board and central office personnel: twice the number of lockers, half the number of telephones, no assistant principal, a full-time librarian. One principal with a bad back ordered a long-back chair for his office. The response to his request was "that is an assistant superintendent's chair, and if you get one, they'll all want one." But the principal responded to the challenge to his new authority and got his chair. Many anecdotes such as this one will accompany the change.

As pilot schools work out the ways in which they engage in budget planning, derive benefits from their newfound flexibility, and gain feedback from their new accountability, they become a highly credible source of information for the central office and remaining schools. News travels quickly and these schools are watched closely to see if the practices do indeed match the intention of the district policy documents. Is this freedom real or just a set of good intentions? Do schools have actual authority or is this merely an exercise? For the pilots to be genuinely useful to the district, the length of the pilot period must be decided in advance. Those districts that have engaged in a 1-year program have found that span to be a bit short, because planning for full-scale adoption must start only 6 months after the pilots have begun working under decentralization. They are less able to offer advice then they would have been had their experience been longer. Districts with pilot periods of 3 or 4 years, however, may find that the idea loses some impetus. For districts of moderate size, 2 years may be optimal. There is no escaping it: Most persons connected to your district will be affected by decentralization and for certain people, the change will be quite pronounced. For some, it will be downright uncomfortable. The impacts on six main roles are presented.

School Board

In centralized districts, board members usually have no clear knowledge of where money is being spent or results it brings. Our elected officials lack anything resembling a balance sheet, so they respond sometimes by abandoning their role as policymakers and trying to "make a difference" using clear procedures for resources directed to schools. The simple idea that "schools know best" runs contrary to the mindset of some of these officials, whose tendency is to try to control schools precisely. Yet it just does not make sense to require that each school have a fixed amount of professional development time per teacher. Decentralization demands that board members retreat to their role as policymakers, reviewers of budgets, and monitors of general progress. Along these lines, a board member from a decentralized district said,

We are no longer making rules for schools. There is a need to stand back. When you are uncomfortable with school's particular decisions, you must bite your tongue. It is hard to give up things you think kids should have. The board must believe in their schools' competency and decisions. This is a big leap.

For some board members, this will be hard to bear.

Central Office Staff

The district central office is inhabited by many kinds of interesting people. Responsibilities will increase for some associate superintendents. Their job will be to supervise schools directly, being line officers between the superintendent and a cluster of principals (usually consisting of thirty schools in some geographic area of the district). Remember the one-boss rule? Associate superintendents may be given some direct say over school budgets. Although these district administrators have a controlling function over schools, they also have a helping function, enabling principals to find ways to solve problems.

Another group of very important people in the district office consists of those who offer support services to schools or to the district as a whole. This district support staff group often has particular difficulty accommodating decentralization. The school business officer will be asked to give up the privilege to make educational decisions about what resources schools may or may not have. The maintenance supervisor will be asked to transfer authority over school custodians to the building principals. Instead of initiating projects in schools, subject matter specialists will be asked to respond to school requests most of the time. And other support personnel will be asked to clear their school interventions with principals. Such changes entail a great deal of adjustment for many of these persons, who are often much more competent and up-to-date in their specialties than are principals. For some, the change will be seen as a betrayal of faith in their ability to deliver good service. Some may feel that the role shift is too much and they will choose to make career changes. If a user-pay system for central office staff services is contemplated at a later time, the impact on these roles will be even more severe. Yet not all the impact is negative for these people. Some persons in these staff positions are happy to know that when their personal services or those of the people they supervise are requested (and perhaps paid for) by schools, *they are genuinely wanted.* As one central office staff person remarked, "Their power will increase."

Principal

The role most affected by decentralization is clearly that of the school principal. No other person will encounter more change, more need to adjust, and more potential to make a difference both to his or her school and to the way decentralization works at the school level. As one reckoned, "In decision making, everything comes back to the principal." One of the largest changes may be in the way principals plan with teachers, a topic discussed in the next section.

At bottom, what do principals think of school-based management? A survey was undertaken in a large, decentralized district. They saw the leading strengths, in order, as

- a reduction of decisions to the school level with its accompanying flexibility,
- the effectiveness that this flexibility provided them, and
- the increase in school faculty and staff involvement that resulted.

They were quite clear about the weakness, too. For them, the weaknesses were

- the time demands of instituting the idea and the planning it required,
- the lack of resources (the district was undergoing some retrenchment), and
- the stress that decentralization created.

Was the stress caused by the adoption of decentralization or from the need to make hard decisions? The research does not tell us. But overall, principals were very strongly supportive of decentralization. As might be surmised, the principal's role affected the jobs organization of teachers and support staff directly.

Teachers

For many persons, the real action in school-based management is the way in which teachers get a chance to immerse themselves in the critical decisions of resource deployment in their schools.

When schools are organizationally decentralized, principals determine the way in which the planning process proceeds in their schools. They tend to form budget committees consisting mostly of department heads in secondary schools and grade-based teachers in elementary schools. Such committees field many requests from teachers and other school staff. Dollars requested are always in excess of those available, so the budget committees wrestle with their schools' priorities and make recommendations to the principals. The key words in the last sentence are *make recommendations*.

Principals in decentralized districts have found that if they are subject to a controlling vote of their budget committees and the decision made is a bad one, their necks and careers are on the line. The buck has stopped. Because they have the prime responsibility for such decisions, they reserve the right to have authority over them. Be reminded that it is not easy to override a select committee of serious professionals who have made a recommendation with good reasons. Yet the principals feel that they need to retain their right to veto such recommendation. They also have influence over the budget committee; their own priorities are felt there, of course. This reality led one teacher to reflect, "Some of our principal's pet plans are not open to a vote, and administrator time is one of the sacred cows." Most principals, however, welcome the knowledge and careful homework that the committees bring to the budgeting process. These school administrators seldom make the critical decisions on their own. Thus, in a sense, they have rejected strictly collegial decision making, adopted consultative decision making, and rejected autocratic decision making. And to some extent, school-based management becomes department-based or grade-based management.

School administrators may be pleased, but how do teachers in general feel about school-based management? For them, is it a burden or a boon? Generally, they tend to agree with principals. From a survey in a large decentralized district, they said that the four leading advantages (in order) were flexibility, teacher involvement, delegation of decisions to the school level, and an increased awareness of costs. Drawbacks were also evident. In order, they were the time demands of decentralization, a shortage of funds, the stress involved, and—interestingly—the increased authority of the principal. At least some teachers were not happy to have their principals hold a greater influence on the direction of their schools and daily life within them. To a considerable degree, the teachers were supportive of decentralization.

Yet not all teachers wish to participate in budget planning. Many are much more concerned with the instruction of children than with school governance. Teaching is where they receive their satisfaction; they relish seeing the light go on in their kids' eyes when a new understanding dawns. Consequently, it is hard to say how much they should be encouraged to take an interest in school planning. Some, by temperament or because they are inexperienced teachers, will just not want to become involved in resource allocation within their schools. For them, the effects will not be sufficiently dramatic to warrant the effort. Others, though, will welcome the chance to make requests and perhaps to add their voice to the school planning process.

In another survey of a large decentralized district, teachers were asked to offer their reactions to school-based management before and after it was instituted. Those teachers who had not encountered it were quite circumspect, yet those who had experienced it believed that it resulted in improvements to their schools. It was worth the candle.

If the district is decentralized so that teachers are given a discretionary vote on school councils, then it is the faculty who will have the authority to make a good many school policy decisions. Unfortunately, evidence of how such councils function is scant. It is certain, however, that the role boundaries of their authority must be clearly specified in order for them to contribute effectively. Most surely, the question of who is accountable for wrongly made decisions must be weighted before this form of school-based management is implemented.

Support Staff

Not much evidence is available about how the roles of school support staff are affected by decentralization. Remember that each school decides how many support staff members will work in its building and who those individuals will be. Perhaps because support personnel know they are more wanted by their schools (than under centralized arrangements), one supervisor said, "They regard themselves as part of the school team; they take pride in school achievements, have greater self-confidence, and have positive feelings about their involvement." Still, not all are satisfied and some simply do not wish to join in the planning process. For them, their immediate jobs may be more important to them than issues involving overall school direction.

Parents

The role of parents under school-based management will vary greatly depending on whether the district is decentralized organizationally or politically.

Organizational decentralization permits principals to consult with parents, who normally participate in an advisory committee for the school. Principals often assert that such input is ample, partly because many avenues exist for parental input such as volunteering, fund raising, ad hoc committees, and conferences with teachers. Yet, unless the existence of a parental advisory committee is required, parental participation may not increase with decentralization. As John Goodlad (1984) says, many parents do not feel competent to make decisions that must be grounded in the professional knowledge of teachers. Faculty often agree with him.

For some parents, the change to organizational decentralization will reduce their ability to lobby the school board for resources that they think their school needs. When they bring complaints or suggestions to the board, they will be redirected to the school principal. Accustomed to making end runs to the board office, not all will accept this change.

Political decentralization is another matter. With this form, parents form the majority in a controlling committee that has wide authority to direct school policy, including replacing the principal. Elected from the wider parent group, they participate actively in the budgeting process. Their input becomes very important to the direction of the school as well as for its immediate resource allocations for next year. Clearly, the principal's ability to balance the needs of the school as perceived by the professionals and staff with the needs of the school as perceived by the parents becomes an important ingredient in the planning process. When the authority of the school board is felt through the associate superintendent, the principal can be in the position of serving three masters. Perilous.

10   Sabotage at the Trial Stage

Individuals who were most interested in subversion of school-based management at the exploration stage are still around. They know enough about public decision making not to give up, and they continue to be most determined to have the innovation fail. At the trial stage, they have a larger opportunity to undercut the idea than they did when decentralization was just being explored. Now they can capitalize on any negative experiences. Over time, they are growing more determined as decentralization starts to affect them directly. Who are they and what will they try? Let's play an old game and pretend we are in their shoes. Here is the advice that I would give as a devil's advocate.

School Board Members

Some school board members will lobby against the idea of school-based management for rather questionable reasons:

As a school board member with a teaching background,
profess that you know best what's good for schools. Insist
that all schools need a music synthesizer, among other
key items. That way you can continue your interventionist
role with gusto.

You are another board member who wants to derail the
idea of school-based management because you think you
will lose your direct control of schools. Vote to proceed to
the trial stage during retrenchment or labor unrest. The
result? Efforts to decentralize will be strongly associated
with cutbacks or be seen as a weapon management will
use against workers.

In other guises, as a board member who fears the
impending changes, use your position on a school budget
review committee to hammer the first school that wants
twice the normal allowance for computers. Then pound
the first principal who wants to increase class size so
teachers can have preparation time, which is at only 15
minutes per week in her school.

District Administrators

Some district administrators will see decentralization
as a direct threat to their power base:

As a superintendent who really would rather preserve
your own discretion, select only weak principals for your
pilot schools. That way, with luck the experiment will fail
and you can label decentralization unworkable.

What to do if you are a superintendent who would
rather not bother with going through the whole exercise
of an authentic trial of school-based management? Simple. Tolerate opposition to the idea in the form of defiance
among those close to you, thus giving the clear impression that you are too indifferent to implement the idea.

As a superintendent whose district adopted school-based management involuntarily, be sure to permit violation of the key principles of decentralization as the innovation is being tried. For instance, ensure that senior central office employees continue to override school decisions, thus making a mockery of your district's policy statements on decentralization. At the same time, tell school personnel that they have the authority to make decisions.

What if you are an assistant superintendent with lots of goodies to give out? You may be deprived of some of them! Cultivate mistrust and maintain secrecy with regard to the purposes of school-based management. If you are successful, this strategy will reduce open dialogue on the merits and demerits of decentralization.

As a central office planner, make sure that the gap between what schools received last year and what they receive during the first year of school-based management is as large as possible. You can starve some schools while permitting others to have an abundance of resources. Naturally, decentralization will be criticized severely as a result.

Say you are a school business officer who does not want to give up any portion of your power to make decisions about educational matters. Merely impede and obstruct implementation efforts in the pilot schools, thus attempting to ensure failure of the idea.

As a school business officer who is bothered by all the adjustment, proclaim that it is impossible for principals to learn about accounts. Relief is at hand! The fact that you mastered the system boosts your professional stature and decreases decentralization's chances in your district at the same time.

As an associate superintendent who is given the job of overseeing school budgets but who wants to take charge of schools personally, make budgetary review very tight. Permit less than 5% variance from last year's school budgets, thus discouraging schools from trying any novel reallocations.

You are a former principal in the board office who thinks that you may have to return to the schools to work. A scary thought, particularly when there are many new responsibilities to face! Relax. Just insist that principals are incompetent to manage money matters or take charge of maintenance and other specialist employees within their schools. Your opinion has special credibility and others will be happy to support it.

Union Leaders

Some union leaders will see their power to make rules for schools shift to their membership:

You are a teachers' union leader whose political agenda is to cultivate mistrust of teachers with their administrations. Confuse teachers with the role that they are expected to play in decentralization. Insist that they will call all the shots in schools and then feign disappointment when that possibility does not work out. Teacher resentment will build.

As a teachers' union leader who cannot abide by the idea that teachers know what is good for themselves, do not permit any contract violations. With that outlook, you can guarantee certain staffing inflexibilities, thus preventing teachers from getting the staff they want in schools but maintaining your collective agreement to the letter.

Say you are a teachers' union representative and you work with your district to develop school staffing guidelines. The contract will set out minimum staffing requirements for each school, thus ensuring that schools are barely able to change the numbers of persons in each category. With those guidelines in place, you can effectively neutralize the staffing component of decentralization and reduce its scope to equipment and supplies. As a support staff union leader who feels sure that your zone of freedom is threatened, ensure that decentralization is confused with job security so that most personnel will feel that their jobs will be on the line. Paint a portrait of doom and gloom before the district communicates the facts to your membership. First impressions are critical!

Restatement of the Trial Stage

Change is easy to botch. Changing to school-based management is no exception. When the idea is adopted in an unthinking or superficial way, ample confusion and opposition results. The involvement of people is critical to the success of the change. Much local invention and effort are needed. Many districts will drop the ball. Failures are guaranteed to occur in some places. Let's recapitulate some of the critical parts of the trial stage.

At some early point, ideally during the exploration stage but no later than the start of the trial stage, it is necessary to appoint a champion for decentralization, an animator who will provide the spark that kindles imaginations. He or she must assemble lots of information and provide opportunities for others to learn about the ins and outs of decentralization.

Some absolutely critical early decisions have to be made at the trial stage. Your district must choose between two rather separate forms of school-based management. One sets in motion organizational delegation of authority to make many decisions to schools. The other transmits this authority to parent councils that control schools directly. Another major choice is the initial scope of decisions to be accorded to schools. Are schools to be given the say-so over personnel resources or not? Many of the benefits of decentralization as well as the magnitude of the change are affected by the answer to this question. Once these two overarching issues have been resolved, prudence demands that districts draft some policies governing decentralization to provide clarity of intentions and to specify the meaning of the change.

A great deal of information about school-based management should be shared widely among all district employees. The inclusion of all groups is a time-consuming but absolutely necessary part of successful planning. Students, parents, support staff, teachers, principals, central office staff, and board members require involvement. Most critically, interest groups such as unions need to be included and agreements must be reached with them. The problem of balancing employee security with school flexibility of decision making must be addressed directly and resolved.

The method of allocating lump-sum money to schools, mostly based on a simple dollars-per-student amount, will be very important to schools as the formulas will affect their capacity to function. Not difficult to devise or initially elaborate, the formulas should show some adaptation to local school conditions, particularly school size. During the first year, major changes in the resources designated for individual schools should not change greatly in order to make sure that no schools are starved. A committee to monitor the formulas is usually appointed.

More head-scratching will be necessary to develop the overall budgetary planning processes to be followed by the district and its schools. Who does what and when need to fit together as district actions affect school actions and vice versa. Adaptions to the present budgeting cycle need to occur.

An accountability system forms an integral part of school district decentralization. If parents, students, and all district employees are given the opportunity to give honest feedback in summary form, then problems and successes will be duly registered and key actors can agonize over the reports. Planning for annual surveys is much the same for any other large-scale questionnaire. Results should not just be disseminated; rather, the data should be used to help strengthen the performance of programs and personnel.

After extensive preparations, it's time to select some pilot schools to try it. They are usually volunteers and should be credible choices. They will spark a considerable demand for information and also break a number of old rules—thus providing some good tests of the stated principles of decentralization. An optimal pilot period for many districts is 2 years.

Both prior preparation and pilot school activities will make evident the role changes on the part of many key players on the district stage. Board members will need to concern themselves with policy and not be involved with explicit school rules or school particulars. Many central office employees will find themselves in a staff or supportive position rather than in a line position where decisions are made about the quantity and kind of resources that schools are to receive. When the decentralization is organizational in form, persons in line positions will be placed directly in charge of schools. Principals and assistant principals will be affected considerably, being given much more authority to make important staffing and other resource decisions; they will also feel some of the burden of overwork created by decentralization, particularly in that first year, with its trial and error. Teachers will be much more involved in planning, although the nature of their involvement will tend to vary school by school. Faculty will probably support school-based management more after they have tried it than prior to the experience. Support staff will feel more part of the school team but many may be ambivalent. And parents will have much greater involvement if they are active on the parent controlling council when the decentralization is political. Otherwise, their role will not be affected much except that they can direct their concerns to school personnel who are able to deal with more of those problems then they were under centralized administration.

Aside from natural difficulties, objection in principle, and honest mistakes, some will oppose the change to decentralization for their private reasons, usually having to do with self- or group interests. As the trial stage brings the prospect of decentralization much closer, and individuals have their own agendas, some key players will accentuate their efforts to upset the change in a number of inventive ways.

Let's assume that your school board, along with the community of support to be found throughout the district, has determined that the experiment with the pilot schools has been successful. An adoption or rejection decision point has been placed before the board and discussed extensively. Partly on the evidence and partly on faith, the board and other participants have invoked the courage to give the remaining schools the opportunity to experience the benefits of school-based management. The decision is "go" and it is up to you to get ready for the next, sometimes more perilous, stage, where the commitment to decentralization is made and adoption is district-wide. You have moved to the next stage.

STAGE III

COMMITMENT

Your district has decided to adopt school-based management for almost all of its schools. It is now committed to the idea of decentralization, and although the change has been implemented in the pilot schools, there are a great many people out there who still find the idea rather novel. They are the ones who did not volunteer. At the commitment stage, most of the remaining schools are involved. The plan is to help them so that there is minimal confusion and as few mishaps as possible.

11 Further Implementation

Districtwide Preparations

Once the decision is made to continue with school-based management and expand the core of schools that are decentralized, another question arises: What will be the schedule of adoption? The change to a large number of schools can proceed in one of three ways: all at once, phased in, or voluntary.

The *all-at-once* option relies heavily on the ability of the pilot schools and the central office to provide the information and services necessary to scores of schools—100 schools or more—to enter the new era at the same time. A go-for-broke challenge, but it's been done. Naturally, the change is easier if only equipment and supplies are involved. One special advantage of the all-at-once strategy is that it gives much less time for opposition to co-alesce. Once schools try decentralization, they find they like it.

95

The *phased-in* choice permits the pilot schools to teach the earlier schools and the earlier schools to teach the later ones. Cleveland used a clever matching arrangement in which each school that had experienced decentralization was paired with one about to take on the responsibilities of school-based management. As a result, the number of decentralized schools doubled each year. Adaptation to the new order was spread over 4 years.

Schools could be permitted to adopt school-based management *voluntarily*. The rationale is that a voluntary adoption could be much more likely to succeed than an involuntary one. Possibly, though, a number of your schools will never get around to adopting the idea. Those schools will probably be among the ones that could benefit from it the most.

Regardless of the pattern of adoption, the change will produce a lot of anticipation and excitement among many people, but will also cause some central office personnel and principals to "make career decisions." They will find their personal philosophies or abilities to be incompatible with their new tasks. Most likely they will leave the district, change jobs, or retire.

Adventures

A number of good things are likely to happen as more and more schools in your district make their own decisions about resources. One secondary school with 1,000 students and 42 teachers took these actions: reduced class sizes, established a library media center and academic challenge program, and saved $26,000 on utility bills. Some of your schools will emphasize a "back-to-basics" approach, others, innovations such as team teaching. Evidence indicates that decentralized schools will show a greater diversity of curricular offerings and instructional forms than their centralized counterparts.

One corner of the budget that will see a lot of action is the surplus or deficit. Remember, surpluses and deficits can be carried over to the next year. Some schools will be very conservative and salt away surpluses in order to purchase something expensive at a later time. Others will jump in and upgrade their equipment or add personnel, thereby incurring a deficit.

Vigorous budgetary activity tends to dispel two myths about principals at the commitment stage. Widely held by persons in centralized districts, these myths assert that (1) principals are too naive to cope with decisions regarding money and (2) they will turn into technicians (mere managers who will forsake their responsibilities of instructional leadership). When the majority of principals face their responsibilities under decentralization, however, not only do they find themselves equal to the job of financial management, but they go on to assert that they are more empowered as educational leaders. This is because the tasks of learning and the resources for learning are brought together. Besides, who ever heard of an important school decision requiring no resources?

Are these new responsibilities welcomed by the majority of principals? You bet. Although their ability to pass the buck had been stripped away, two surveys in a decentralized district showed principals' support for school-based management. One demonstrated that principals had a much higher level of satisfaction with their jobs than those in the surrounding centralized districts. Another showed that 79% of the principals in the decentralized district who responded said that they would recommend that other districts consider school-based management. Moreover, teachers became more appreciative of decentralization as time progressed, though they were often unwilling to participate in decisions in which they had no personal stake.

One source of principal and teacher satisfaction in
districts that become organizationally decentralized will
probably stem from the manner in which teachers contribute to the planning process. When teachers are consulted via budgetary committees, they have their say and
the principal receives valuable input for decisions that he
or she may be incompetent to make on his or her own.
Those principals who start their planning in an authori-
tarian way may find themselves moving to a consultative
mode for these reasons. In all likelihood, they will stop at
consultation and not move to a collegial model, for the
reason given by this principal: "If I involve my teachers in
everything and don't make my own decisions, it may
create an impression that I do not know my job and I
cannot make the decisions that I am paid to make." This
quotation suggests that teachers may want selective involvement, depending on the kinds of decisions to be
made.

What about the involvement of others in budgeting?
Quite possibly, but not assuredly, support staff members
and parents will be invited to have input as well. Naturally, when the district is politically decentralized, teachers or parents not only have preferences concerning the
planning process—they have control of it.

Misadventures

When decentralization is adopted districtwide, the experiences of a large array of schools will emerge. Although
the pilots provided some clear indication of what the
problems would be, they could never predict the full range
of difficulties encountered. Here are some illustrations.

Schools may find ways to subvert the allocation process, as an example from one district will show. When

the allocation formula for utilities was being set up, it worked in the following way. Next year's dollars for each school were to be based on an average of the heating expenses for 3 years: 2 years previously, 1 year previously, and the current year. A few schools considered this arrangement to be a grand opportunity. They threw open their windows and doors to the winter winds and influenced their heating costs accordingly.

Some schools, and particularly the principals in them, will be afraid of establishing priorities and making decisions regarding money. They do not want the authority to make the important decisions about personnel and other resources that have an impact on learning. They would rather chastise the central office for what can't be done and get by as usual. Often this fear will produce a kind of lethargy. These principals will complain that they were never made properly ready—specifically, that there was not enough orientation and training in budgeting and accounting. Some of their gripes will be justified; it seems that no one is ever fully prepared for a change of this size, though some principals will address it with gusto. Other school personnel will disagree with school-based management in principle. It is important that these people have their day in court and are fully informed about what is known concerning decentralization. The fact is, misunderstanding produces fear and foot-dragging.

Here is a small example of what can go wrong. In a decentralized district, a principal decided to reduce her custodian's hours by 15%. She received clearance from the maintenance supervisor, the custodial supervisor, and the custodian himself, though he changed his mind after he spoke to his union. The union's response was to have the water turned off in the part of the building affected. Naturally, the pipes froze. It appears that the union was not sufficiently included in the decentralization plan.

Let's assume that most schools get on with the job of planning their budgets for the next school year. Everything seems to be going grandly, but then another problem may surface. Remarkable as it may seem, those in schools may find it hard to assume power. Many principals may not believe that they have the authority to make such decisions, even when given the clearance to do so. They will still behave in the standard fashion, not exercising their freedom. It may take a year or two before those in the trenches believe the rhetoric and proclamations that they have the authority to make requests that were invariably turned down under centralization. What's more, they may remark that it took a year for them to realize that school-based management was more than some accountant's game with endless numbers. For many, the preoccupation with keeping the books straight will be much more immediate than asking what resources are desirable. Despite the best planning, sometimes people will lose sight of the forest for the trees. At one principals' meeting, discussion turned to custodial supplies. The principals devoted 30 minutes to the merits of hand towels, blow dryers, and different kinds of toilet paper.

Assuming that the bookkeeping is in order, there will still be difficulties with the planning process itself. Budget committees must be struck and they will take a year or so to learn what their tasks are and how to accomplish them. Not everybody will be happy with their recommendations; some teachers may complain that they have been treated badly. Committee composition can also be a problem. Logically, support staff members have much information to offer, but if they are invited, teachers may question why secretaries and aides have input into decisions about class sizes. And these committees will work rather hard and put in long hours. They will be concerned about enrollment projections, calculations of costs, and the ranges of academic and other goals. Further, they will be approached by teachers and others with special requests. Not all will be gratified with the sequence of events, as illustrated by this gripe from a principal under decentralization:

> My teachers and I were unhappy with the fact that schools were required to prepare their budgets at the wrong time of the year. The task of preparing a school's budget for the ensuing September had to begin in February. How could a teacher plan in February for the class she would not even meet until September? How could a high school plan its program for next year, three months before course registrations have come in? Sometimes we had to redo the budget totally in September as everything could change radically. When this happened, decisions would have to be made so quickly that there was no time for staff involvement.

Although such difficulties are not universal, they will be encountered. Sometimes teachers and principals disagree over what should receive the attention in budget committees. This disparity led one teacher to wonder if the principal was more concerned with the boilers or with the kids. The tendency on the part of a few principals to preoccupy themselves with noneducation matters will surface. When it does, probably the need is apparent for some coaching on the part of the associate superintendent.

A problem that will arise after the budgeting effort is one of principal accountability. As principals are to be held accountable for the results of the decisions made in their schools, the question arises: To what extent? This problem was well stated by a principal under school-based management:

> The quality and nature of the significant inputs such as students and teachers are often not controlled by the principal. Principals may be in a position to control resources but they are the least significant of the inputs. Is

it reasonable then, to give principals control of such a small portion of the inputs and then to hold them accountable for the outputs?

That concern speaks directly to the methods of personnel evaluation for principals. Despite their best efforts, principals are not always called to account for their spending practices. One principal received a lucky transfer. His school had a 15% budget deficit that was inherited by his replacement. How far is accountability to be pushed? The question cries out for a response.

Prospects for Recentralization

The possibility that your district will recentralize sometime during the commitment stage is dependent on two main factors: the advent of retrenchment and the extent of opposition. In a number of districts, financial problems have precipitated a collapse of decentralized management. Dollars diminish and employees must be laid off. But who decides who stays and who goes? It is often easier to make decisions centrally under such conditions. Besides, the implementation of school-based management becomes confused with retrenchment. One principal shared a perception widely held in his district during a time of financial cutbacks: "Decentralization is a way to decentralize the agony."

The other threat to decentralization is the opposition to it, always resident in the district and often located within the central office, among the group of inhabitants of staff positions in central offices often called "the blob." Usually, they have been recruited from the teaching ranks in order to carry out functions that the district believes are important for all schools. Frequently called coordinators

or supervisors and sometimes assistant superintendents, they provide expert advice, inspire teachers, and
keep very much up-to-date in their subject or field. They
have money for special programs and are called on to do
a great many tasks. Among the most talented persons in
the district, they are sensitive to the "larger picture" of
districtwide needs, which schools often ignore. They carry
out many districtwide initiatives. However, their presence
in the district office creates some problems.

These central office staff persons have no direct responsibilities for children's learning. Because their services
are not always wanted when given to schools, they are
not seen as accountable to anyone. As one associate
superintendent said, "They may spend their afternoons
in the park for all we know." In some districts, their
numbers can be quite large. When the ratio of pupils to
professionals in a district is 16 to 1 and class sizes are
32 pupils to 1 teacher, there is a "phantom person," a
blob member whose role is to help the teacher but who
is usually not there when needed. When districts decentralize, such functionaries in the blob may oppose
school-based management because their roles are dimin-
ished and sometimes eliminated. The possibility of significant role changes is enhanced if the district considers
moving to a user-pay arrangement for central office staff.
Their opposition can be particularly effective if key sup-
porters of school-based management leave the district at
the commitment stage.

Conspiracies at the Commitment Stage

At this point, the full force of decentralization is felt
on those who oppose it for reasons of maintaining their
power. This stage may be their last chance to mount

effective opposition. Let's pretend we are in their shoes and contemplate a few of the more ingenious ways that they will try, or continue to try, to thwart the innovation.

As a school board member who is unhappy with school-based management, you observe that although the board has incurred a considerable budget deficit, school surpluses are substantial and would make up your short-fall nicely. Super! Just vote to confiscate school surpluses to cover the district deficit. If a majority votes in your favor, you will ensure that there will never be school surpluses again.

You are an associate superintendent of curriculum whose empire is threatened by decentralization. Consider a palace revolt. Conspire with others who stand to lose power and dig up all the bad decisions schools have made. Lead the charge with that evidence and try to depose the king. If the insurrection works, you will be first in the line of succession to the throne. If the rebellion fails, seek other jobs in safer, centralized realms.

As a maintenance department head, fight furiously for your right to make decisions that have been designated as school-based. This action will create ample conflict with principals, confuse the maintenance personnel, and probably precipitate union grievances. Decentralization can be blamed for the change from tranquility to combat conditions.

You are a school business officer quite hostile to decentralization. Use retrenchment as an excuse to advocate recentralization, indicating that cutbacks require quick action. There is nothing like the fear of job losses to produce a desire on the part of many persons in schools and in central offices to have the central office take the heat. If your plan works, discretionary budgets can be recalled and cuts made. By the time the storm is over, school-based management will be forgotten.

Restatement of the Commitment Stage

In brief, the commitment stage involves the need to prepare for districtwide adoption of decentralization. The schedule is critical. You can

- adopt for all schools at once,
- adopt for schools in a phased-in pattern, or
- permit schools to adopt voluntarily.

Although most personnel will be willing to work toward the adoption, others will look for positions elsewhere. No one is indispensable; the district will be able to cope without them.

At this stage, you may expect more rules to be broken, battles to be won, and stories to be told. Schools will behave somewhat unpredictably, particularly with the use of their surpluses and deficits. Your principals will find that they can handle the load and that they do not turn into technicians. Most principals will strongly endorse the change and most teachers will support it, though less positively, once they have tried it. The usual model of school planning will be one in which teachers and others are consulted as the budget is prepared.

Problems will emerge, too. The less competent and decision-averse principals will have a hard time. Many principals will simply not believe their newfound freedom and so will not take advantage of it initially. Schools will formulate budget committees, but they will make mistakes as they learn a process that is very new for them. Planning will be difficult for some schools. And principal evaluation will have to be examined in light of the new responsibilities.

What are the chances of recentralization in your district? They depend on at least two factors: the advent of

retrenchment and the extent that opposition has solidi-
fied. In the past, opposition often has been rooted in the
central office among those who see their position about
to erode. Some likely tactics of these people have been
illustrated.

12 Capstone Comments

Decentralization offers the prospect that schools may be improved so that they can better serve the needs of the children who learn within them. They can also help to make those who work inside them more effective and more satisfied. Naturally, the more school-based management your district has, the stronger its effects will be. When 65% to 85% of district operating budgets go to schools, lots of good things can happen. It is possible to combine instructional leadership with the resources required to do the job. For years, school administrators have been plagued by the image of Mr. Weatherbee, the ineffectual principal in the Archie comic. He never achieved very much. Principals can now do a lot more. Goodbye, Mr. Weatherbee!

This guidebook has told the story of a journey. It is organized around the three important stages that districts go through on their way to decentralization. These are exploration, where information on school-based management is gathered; trial, where the idea is tested; and commitment, where the entire district is immersed in the process. How long will adoption take? If 1 year is taken for exploration, 2 for trial, and 2 more for commitment, 5 years is a reasonable estimate. To what avail?

Let's recall the main goals of school-based management. School district decentralization aims to improve and empower schools in three main ways. It offers flexibility of decision making with regard to the kind and amount of resources needed for education. It provides a measure of accountability to the public, who are told more directly how the money is spent. And it offers the potential of greater productivity in the form of increased learning and both parental and student satisfaction. By directing resources to the schools (as the dollar follows the child), it is a way to speak to the problem of the blob, where an excess of dollars is allocated to headquarters personnel in centralized districts. Further, it may be used to give parents and teachers more direct control of schools. In short, decentralization is one way of restructuring school districts.

Yet honesty demands that we look at an idea thoroughly and prepare well for the major change if we decide to adopt it. Many pitfalls await along the way, and now is the time to discover as many as you can. It is most important that the idea not be oversold. If it is touted as the source of all good changes in education, there will be many failures and decentralization will rightfully go the way of other educational fads.

Decentralization requires that you believe in your fellow human beings. In order to trust people, you must have faith in them. As an optimistic view of human life, these ideas suggest that educators have the interests of their students at heart. In small numbers, they will do what they are paid to do when held accountable. Such beliefs are not to be faulted when individuals make mistakes. In short, evidence suggests that school-based management can work if given the opportunity.

There are always reasons for centers.
Some are well established, such as centers for
egocentrism, ethnocentrism, and heliocentrism.
Being near the center of buoyancy
or the center of gravity seems a good idea,
All like to be centerpieces and at center stage.
They strongly favor centralization
and are usually inhabited by centroids,
though centaurs are welcomed.
Being the center of the action,
they rotate around the epicenter,
and that causes a problem.

The central concern I wish to raise
is the center of mass of the
accumulated central offices.
Central to the problem is
the centripetal forces
to which they are subjected.
Some of the centers may be
at the center of a black hole. They require
all correspondence to be center-justified,
all activities to be front and center
and all thinking to be properly centrist.
To be left or right of center
is to be quite peripheral.
But some centers are way out in center field.
While not wishing to appear unduly concentric,
I want to point out the existence of the dead center.
The center of the problem is what we all know:
that the center cannot hold.
What we need is a good centerpunch
or placement of centers in a centrifuge
so that we no longer become "centerbored."
Some proper action must be undertaken
to make a center fold.
Then the axis of centrality might give way
and schools could revolve around

more off-center pursuits

D.J.B.

Figure 12.1. Centrally Speaking

Some districts can find the courage to change their structure and offer their children the potential for a better education. Is yours one of them?

Selected References

Brown, Daniel J. (1990). *Decentralization and school-based management*. London: Taylor & Francis/Falmer Press.

Caldwell, B., & Spinks, J. (1988). *The self-managing school*. London: Taylor & Francis/Falmer Press.

Carnegie Forum on Education and the Economy. (1988) *A nation prepared: Teachers for the twenty-first century*. New York: Author.

Cuban, L. (1990). Reforming again, again, and again. *Educational Researcher, 19*(1), 3-13.

Drucker, P. (1986). *The frontiers of management*. New York: E. P. Dutton.

Edmonds, R. (1979). Effective schools for the urban poor. *Educational Leadership, 37*(1), 16.

Elmore, R. F., & Associates. (1990). *Restructuring schools*. San Francisco: Jossey-Bass.

Fullan, M. (1982). *The meaning of educational change*. Toronto: Ontario Institute for Studies in Education.

Glickman, C. D. (1990). Pushing school reform to a new edge: The seven ironies of empowerment. *Phi Delta Kappan, 72*(1), 68-75.

Goodlad, J. I. (1984). *A place called school*. New York: McGraw-Hill.

Greenhalgh, J. (1984). *School site budgeting*. Lanham, MD: University Press of America.

Hess, F. (1991). *School restructuring: Chicago style*. Newbury Park, CA: Corwin Press/Sage.

Huberman, A. M., & Crandall, D. P. (1982). *People, policies, and practices: Examine the chain of social improvement. Vol. 9: Implications for action*. Andover, MA: The Network.

Kogan, M. (1986). *Educational accountability: An analytic overview*. London: Hutchinson and Co.

Lieberman, A., & Miller, L. (1990). Restructuring schools: what matters and What works. *Phi Delta Kappan, 71*(10), 759-764.

Marburger, C. L. (1985). *One school at a time: School-based management, a process of change.* Columbia, MD: National Committee for Citizens in Education.

Mintzberg, H. (1983). *Structure in fives: Designing effective organizations.* Englewood Cliffs, NJ: Prentice-Hall.

Peters, T. J., & Waterman, R. H., Jr. (1982). *In search of excellence: Lessons from America's best-run companies.* New York: Harper & Row.

Purkey, S. C., & Smith, M. S. (1983). Effective schools: A review. *Elementary School Journal, 83*(4), 427-452.

Sources of Further Information

Particularly at the exploration stage, educators and policymakers need to rely on a broad base of information and not just a single source, this guidebook included. Visits to districts that have achieved or are experimenting with decentralization are most beneficial. At present, some major ones include Edmonton, Alberta; Chicago, Illinois; Cleveland, Ohio; Tulsa, Oklahoma; and Dade County, Florida. Conferences in which administrative topics are discussed, such as the American Association of School Administrators, often produce a useful sharing of ideas and papers to bring home.

Another helpful avenue for learning about school-based management is the use of experts. They tend to be of two kinds. One consists of those who have studied or read widely about decentralization—they are useful at the exploration stage to give district personnel some idea of what school-based management is and how it works. The other set includes people from decentralized districts, particularly principals, who can relate their personal experiences and respond well to detailed questions about problems, real or imagined. As outsiders, both can speak freely about the strengths and weaknesses of decentralization, all without worrying about local agendas.

Many periodicals have restructuring as a recurrent theme. Among them are the *Phi Delta Kappan*, the *American School Board Journal*, *Principal*, *Educational Leadership*, and the *NASSP Bulletin*. Unfortunately, most of the articles one reads are wholly positive about school-based management. Authors appear convinced that it will revolutionize education, but that potential has yet to be demonstrated. One way to separate the more valid sources from the frivolous is to look for articles that are grounded in research. Even if they are not well crafted, they at least base their conclusions on evidence rather than just opinion. For an in-depth review of organizational decentralization, see Brown (1990). It is most important to make an informed decision to restructure or not with the full knowledge of the triumphs and mistakes of others, to know both the promises and the pitfalls of decentralization.

Index